"*Shock Waves* shines a light on tl
honors their own tattered spirit
the art of self-care and how to couple it with caring."

—Patricia Weaver Francisco, author of
Telling: A Memoir of Rape and Recovery

"An honest and hopeful approach to the important and challenging
work of traumatic loss."

—Thomas M. Ellis, director of the Center for Grief, Loss &
Transition and author of *This Thing Called Grief*

"With the earnestness of a teacher, the compassion of a healer, and
the credibility of a partner living alongside someone with PTSD,
Cynthia Orange has written a truly useful book. She leaves us with
the conviction that self-care is not a lofty or selfish goal, but a necessity when in relationship with someone who has PTSD. The story
of her own family's healing is a boon to the soul."

—Julie E. Neraas, author of *Apprenticed to Hope:
A Sourcebook for Difficult Times*

"Cynthia Orange has written a wise, well-researched, and moving
book for victims of PTSD and their loved ones. Hers is the voice
of hard-earned wisdom from personal journey. I was moved to
tears by the authenticity of this honest book."

—Ann Linnea, author of *Deep Water Passage*
and *Keepers of the Trees*

"*Shock Waves* is filled with wise and down-on-the-ground suggestions for dealing with this pervasive problem in our culture. It is also
the story of the author's own struggle with her husband's PTSD,
narrated with a candor that does not flinch before the heartache
and difficulties this disorder represents. Orange offers a next step for
those stopped in their tracks, and a realistic hope for those who now
can only see the darkness."

—Dr. Tex Sample, au   *Earthy Mysticism*

Shock Waves

A Practical Guide
to Living with a Loved One's PTSD

Cynthia Orange

Hazelden
Center City, Minnesota 55012
hazelden.org

Library of Congress Cataloging-in-Publication Data

Orange, Cynthia.
    Shock waves : a practical guide to living with a loved one's PTSD / by Cynthia Orange.
        p.   cm.
    Includes bibliographical references.
    ISBN 978-1-59285-856-9 (softcover)
        1. Post-traumatic stress disorder—Patients—Family relationships.   2. Post-traumatic stress disorder—Diagnosis.   3. Stress management.   4. Self-care, Health.   I. Title.
    RC552.P67O73 2010
    616.85'21—dc22   2010005721

Editor's note
The names, details, and circumstances may have been changed to protect the privacy of those mentioned in this publication.
    This publication is not intended as a substitute for the advice of health care professionals.
    Alcoholics Anonymous and AA are registered trademarks of Alcoholics Anonymous World Services, Inc.

13 12 11 10   1 2 3 4 5 6

Cover design by Percolator
Interior design by David Spohn
Typesetting by BookMobile Design and Publishing Services

Author's Note

THE STORIES EXCERPTED throughout this book are based on actual experiences, relayed to me through interviews and conversations or in response to questionnaires distributed to trauma survivors; to those affected by a loved one's trauma or PTSD; and to therapists, doctors, addiction counselors, or others who work with trauma survivors and those affected by a loved one's trauma or PTSD. Unless otherwise noted, they are presented anonymously to protect the privacy of the people involved. In some cases, some details have been changed to ensure anonymity.

I have intentionally employed the University of Oxford convention of using "they," "them," or "their" with a singular noun such as "loved one," to ensure gender inclusiveness while avoiding the more formal and awkward use of "he or she," "his or her," or "him or her."

For Jessica, Jeff, Oskar, Quinlan, and Michael
The family I treasure; the future I embrace

Contents

Preface

ALTHOUGH IT SOUNDS LIKE A B MOVIE, our story began in the summer of 1968, at the top of the Empire State Building. I was visiting New York with two girlfriends from Minnesota, and Michael was there with several of his seminary high-school friends from Ohio. Our faces were smooth with youthful anticipation, our lives fairly uncomplicated. We felt an instant connection, and I came home and announced to my best friend, "I met the man I know I could happily marry." Then he went off to march in the Vietnam War and I marched against it but our friendship remained unshakable; our correspondence honest and constant. Meanwhile, I married someone else, gave birth to a beautiful daughter, and later divorced. When Michael moved to Minnesota in 1973, I finally married my soul mate. He adopted Jessica, and we became an "official" family. I soon discovered, however, that when I married Michael, I also married Vietnam and the trauma he carried from his combat experience.

This book is about our journey and the journeys of others who, like us, have learned to live with the challenges and scars of trauma and the "shock wave" effects of post-traumatic stress disorder (PTSD). While our family's trauma stemmed from war, there are many other causes for trauma, from physical and sexual abuse and violence, to economic and natural disasters, serious accidents, sudden deaths, and terrorist attacks. As my family learned, when trauma affects a loved one, it affects the entire family.

Shock Waves is especially for those who, in their efforts to understand and care for their traumatized love one, discover they need care and understanding themselves. *Shock Waves* is a story of healing and healers. Most important, it is a story of hope.

Acknowledgments

ALTHOUGH I DID NOT EXPECT IT, writing *Shock Waves* has been a cathartic step in an ongoing voyage of healing. I want to thank my family of friends who supported me and this book by telling their stories and helping me gather those of others—stories that poignantly show how far-reaching the effects of trauma can be. I am indebted to all who contributed, and I thank them for their candor and courage in revisiting events and experiences that can still cause pain and sorrow. Know that your wise and hope-filled words make a difference.

Special thanks to my sister Dianne Smith, and to dear friends Rick and Sharon Slettehaugh for their sharp eyes, open hearts, and honest critiques as they read each draft of each chapter. You never fail to make my work better, my life richer.

Thanks also to Chris Hiben for mysteriously intuiting when I needed to cry, laugh, talk, or play. To Vince Hyman and Mary Brennan for sage advice and Fireside chats.

I am forever grateful to Dianna Diers for her listening ears, wise counsel, consistent support, and deep friendship. Thanks also to Patrick, Sandy, and Sean—healers all. You've graced our lives by giving us strength and guidance when we most needed it.

Thanks to Sid Farrar and Richard Solly at Hazelden who shared my vision for this book and helped it become a reality. Hazelden has been an integral part of my writing life for twenty-five years. I so value the friends I've made there and the important and necessary work they do.

Warm thanks to my editor, Pat Boland, for her artful hand in shaping this book. Your expertise made the process painless, and it was pure pleasure getting to know you as we worked together.

My unconditional love and heart-felt thanks to our daughter, Jessica, who stood strong in the midst of our family's struggles with PTSD.

And finally, I wish to thank Michael—my husband, my soul mate, my partner in life and love. I am awed by your courage and the hard work you keep doing to heal from the wounds of war and to so tirelessly work now for peace. This is our story, and throughout its telling you stood by me—always encouraging me to tell our truths in the hope that this book will help others. I love you more genuinely today than I ever have, and look forward to sharing all our tomorrows.

Introduction

If each day falls
inside each night,
there exists a well
where clarity is imprisoned.

We need to sit on the rim
of the well of darkness
and fish for fallen light
with patience.

—PABLO NERUDA*

The word *trauma* comes from the Greek word for *wound,* and some of the wounds that trauma causes are deep and long lasting, creating, as the title to this book suggests, *shock waves* throughout an entire family system. Throughout these pages, trauma survivors and those affected by a loved one's trauma talk about their experiences and candidly offer what worked for them, and what did not. I believe we learn best through stories, and I am

---

*Pablo Neruda, ["If each day falls . . ."], translated by William O'Daly, from *The Sea and the Bells.* Copyright © 1973 by Pablo Neruda and the Heirs of Pablo Neruda. Translation copyright © 1988, 2002 by William O'Daly. Reprinted with permission of Copper Canyon Press, www.coppercanyonpress.org.

forever grateful for the wise and courageous voices heard in this book. It was difficult for these men and women to share their stories of pain and healing, but they told them in order to help others. I am thankful beyond measure that so many have reached safe harbor. So take heart. These are stories of hope from those who have caught that "fallen light."

A traumatic event is one that causes great stress and distress—either physical or emotional, or both—and children, teenagers, men, and women from all walks of life are exposed to trauma every day. According to the National Center for PTSD, in the United States, about 60 percent of men and 50 percent of women experience, witness, or are affected by a traumatic event in their lifetimes. In writing this book, I talked with and heard from people affected by natural disasters and terrorist events—war, rape and other violence, plane crashes, campus killings, serious accidents, the loss of a child—and from those whose lives were turned upside down by a critical illness or a sudden death.

We may think that truly traumatic events need to be as dramatic as childhood sexual abuse or war. Yet many people experience long-term trauma symptoms as a result of deaths in their families, accidents, natural disasters, or other significant occurrences. Some experts also report trauma symptoms among people who are losing jobs, retirement savings, pensions, and their homes in these days of economic crisis. To highlight one type or cause of trauma over another risks creating a hierarchy of suffering that I seek to avoid in this book. To say one experience or story is not as bad as another is to diminish the person and the pain. As the spouse of a survivor of the Oklahoma City bombing put it, "You just can't quantify grief."

Sudden and overwhelming disasters or traumatic events can take a significant emotional toll on survivors, families, and friends. Feelings—for both trauma survivors and loved ones—can become intense and unpredictable. It is normal to experience fear, anxiety, or a sense of helplessness. Some survivors might be more irritable than usual. Others might be angry or suspicious. Some people may have trouble sleeping, concentrating, or remembering things. It is also common to feel an overriding loss of safety and a need for reassurance that loved ones are all right. Some people react immediately, while others have delayed reactions. All these are very normal responses to an abnormal event, and there is no magic formula that can predict when such unsettling feelings will subside.

Research shows that among those affected by a traumatic event, about 8 percent of men and 20 percent of women may develop post-traumatic stress disorder (PTSD)—a life-altering anxiety disorder with symptoms that last over a month. It is the degree and duration of impairment that distinguishes normal reactions to trauma from PTSD. It was normal, for example, to be afraid to fly after the September 11, 2001, terrorist attacks. It would be another thing, however, if you had to quit your job because you were terrified to travel or you couldn't sleep because of night terrors long after 9/11. Some people, such as first responders or others who repeatedly witness trauma, can also develop PTSD. As Stephen R. Paige, Ph.D., so succinctly put it in his peer-reviewed article for eMedicineHealth, "Simply put, PTSD is a state in which you 'can't stop remembering.'"

What is not reflected in statistics about trauma are the millions of loved ones affected by what I call "trickle-down" trauma. Like alcoholism, which is often called a "family* disease," trauma and PTSD can take a devastating toll on friends and family. Living in a household affected by trauma and PTSD is a bit like trying to swim through mud. With the appropriate help, love, and support, however, families can find clearer water.

My husband dreamed about Vietnam almost every night when we were first married. I'd lie close, match my breathing to his, and wait until his breaths seemed smooth, his sleep restful. But still the ghosts of that war slept between us. When he awakened from a

---

*Throughout this book, I use "family" in an inclusive sense to represent not only family and extended family, but also significant others and friends affected by a loved one's trauma.

nightmare, trembling and sullen, he shrugged it off as "just a bad dream." And when this otherwise gentle man exploded with uncharacteristic rage and stalked off lest he strike me, I would be filled with remorse, wondering what I had done to spark such anger. After these infrequent outbursts, I would ask what he was feeling. Michael would usually say "nothing," or look vacant, not able to identify or name his feelings.

I remember pressing him to talk with someone at the VA (Department of Veterans Affairs) after a particularly disturbing nightmare late in the 1970s—before PTSD was a diagnosable condition. He acquiesced, but came home after the visit claiming he was fine, adding that he felt guilty for even going after seeing all the vets at the VA who were "really messed up and really needed help." But he wasn't all right.

Michael tried to shut out ghosts and memories by burying himself in his job as a city planner and exercising compulsively. When our marriage was in trouble and we sought counseling, he blamed his workaholism, not Vietnam. And then came 9/11, the "Shock and Awe" of the United States' bombing of Iraq in 2003, and the images of brave troops with boots on the ground and rifles in hand. This was followed with news that his best friend while in Vietnam had committed suicide by dousing himself with gasoline and lighting a match after leaving a fourteen-page suicide note about his combat experience—an experience Michael had shared. Finally, after decades of trying his best to explain away, ignore, or stuff what we now know were trauma symptoms, Michael was diagnosed with PTSD. He got a medical leave from work, and his healing—and our family's healing—began.

PTSD is a diagnosis that changes as experts continue to learn more about the effects of severe trauma. It is a useful, but at times confusing, measurement tool. In researching this book, I met many trauma survivors who were not officially diagnosed with PTSD. Some experienced the trauma decades ago (before there was a diagnosis for PTSD), yet their symptoms continue. Some, like the survivors of childhood sexual abuse, may not have remembered the trauma until they were adults, and by then may have discounted their trauma reactions by shrugging them off, thinking, "It's just the way I am." Some with many classic symptoms never sought professional help. Others masked their symptoms with alcohol and other drugs. Still others may not have exhibited or disclosed all the symptoms necessary for a diagnosis when they did seek professional advice. Nonetheless, they struggle with the consequences of trauma, and their families usually struggle with them.

I began this book on the eve of our thirty-sixth wedding anniversary. With our lives richer and our days more joyous than ever, it is not easy to sit again on the "rim of the well of darkness" that the poet Neruda describes so well in the poem at the beginning of this introduction, but it feels necessary. In her book *Telling: A Memoir of Rape and Recovery,* Patricia Weaver Francisco addresses the tension that exists when one is filled with both a desire to forget and an obligation to remember. "It is easier to gaze out this sunny window and imagine a world at peace with itself than to look at these memories. I resist, and you who are reading may want to resist. Why go into it then? There are a million sad stories and only one day like this, balmy and just right . . . Why talk about rape when it makes everyone uncomfortable . . . Why not just go on hoping tomorrow will be a better day? Because perfect days are built on difficult mornings."

I, of course, wish that my husband had been spared his traumatic experience. I wish that Francisco and the millions of men and women like her hadn't suffered sexual abuse or other traumas. Trauma symptoms are like party crashers who sneak in just when things are going smoothly in a household. But if family members get better informed about the effects of trauma, learn how to talk about it, discover what can trigger symptoms, and get help in sorting out everyday reactions and behaviors from trauma-related behaviors and feelings, they are better able to expose these wily intruders.

With hard work, good self-care, the love of a supportive community, and help from the appropriate professionals when it is needed, families learn the difference between "getting over" trauma and "working through" the effects of trauma. Sometimes the process of working through means learning to feel again, including the pain. It makes sense that trauma sufferers often stuff emotions or numb uncomfortable feelings, and that their loved ones sometimes adopt these same unhelpful behaviors. But when we can't feel pain, we usually can't feel joy either.

I remember a story about how Kirk Douglas had a stroke that left him unable to speak. In suicidal despair over being a famous actor with no voice, he loaded the gun he had used in his 1957 film with Burt Lancaster, *Gunfight at the O.K. Corral.* When he stuck the gun inside his mouth intending to pull the trigger, the barrel bumped a sensitive tooth, and the alarming pain caused him to reflexively remove the pistol. As Kirk Douglas discovered, sometimes feeling pain can save your life. He eventually learned how to speak again and became an advocate for stroke victims. Like many who survive and learn to integrate the effects of trauma, Douglas said his life—even in his eighties—was filled with new beginnings.

As I stress in chapter 1, "Trauma Responses and PTSD: Normal Reactions to Abnormal Events," post-traumatic symptoms are normal reactions to abnormal events, but the shock waves that trauma sends out can tear families apart if they don't take care of themselves and get the help they all need. Ernest Hemingway wrote, "The world breaks everyone and afterward many are strong at the broken places." Chapter 2, "Acknowledging Loss and Honoring Grief," emphasizes the necessity of mourning what we and our loved ones have lost in the wake of trauma.

Because we received the support we needed and connected with experts who helped us understand what PTSD is and how trauma can affect all family members, we are stronger as individuals and as a family. Taking care of yourself as you struggle to navigate the tumultuous waters of a loved one's trauma or PTSD is not easy, but it is essential—which is why much of this book focuses on self-care for those who love and care for trauma survivors. To extend the water metaphor a bit, taking care of self is like damming a river for power production. In times of drought, the river flows slowly or not at all. A dam collects the water and creates an energy reserve so power can be tapped as it is needed. This is what self-care is all about. When we take good care of ourselves, we create a reservoir of energy, patience, and love that will be there when we need it. Chapter 3, "What about Me? The Importance of Self-Care," offers ways in which readers can balance personal needs and care-giving responsibilities.

One of the goals of this book is to help readers expand their circles of support. When we seek help, we model for children that such an action is healthy and positive, giving them permission to ask for guidance. Chapter 4, "Self-Care II: Toward Healthy Interdependence and Dialogue," discusses the importance of mutual support groups, friends, and healthy activities that provide interaction and support outside the home. Chapter 5, "Self-Care III: Declaring a 'Toxic-Free' Zone," suggests ways to deal with anger. At the end of the book, I have included a list of helpful organizations, books, Web sites, and other resources.

When Michael was diagnosed with PTSD, I felt a surge of relief that at last we could name the unspeakable. At the time of his diagnosis, I had worked as a writer in the area of addiction and recovery for almost twenty years. It helped me immensely to look at Michael's trauma and PTSD through the lens of the Twelve Steps, because the Steps provide such practical tools that help individuals accept what they cannot control—whether or not they belong to a recovery group. While it is not uncommon for trauma sufferers to try to numb themselves with alcohol or other drugs, substance abuse can also be a problem for other family members who struggle to support their loved one. In chapter 6, "Trauma and Addiction: Weathering the Storms," I discuss co-occurring disorders and related issues and have included suggestions on how the Twelve Steps can be used as a healing tool.

Good self-care is particularly important for parents in trauma-stressed families so they are better able to raise resilient children. Chapter 7, "Trauma and Parenting," discusses the effects of trauma on children and offers ways in which parents can provide security and stability in the midst of its aftereffects. In chapter 7, I have included prevention strategies, communication tips, a discussion and examples of "teachable moments," and resources for support.

In chapter 8, "Rebuilding Your Life," I talk about living and growing in trauma's wake. Eventually, Michael learned from his memories instead of being imprisoned by them, and because he and I now have a better understanding of how trauma affects families and can talk about how it has affected our own, our partnership is stronger. We are more honest with each other now and better able to accept responsibility for our own actions and reactions. We laugh more, relax and play more, and when we argue, we fight more fairly. When trauma symptoms appear, as they occasionally still do, we are better able to identify them as responses, not character defects.

Our family continues to grow healthier, but every day there are more families who struggle as we did to stay afloat in the tsunami that is trauma. Michael and I are both committed to doing what we can to help them.

If you are reading this book, you have probably been touched by trauma or know someone who has been. I applaud you for tending your wounds; for having the strength to pick up a book and learn more about trauma. Knowledge is an important step in healing, and it is a step *forward*. It is my wish that you will find hope and comfort in these pages as well as helpful information you can put to use. I hope you will emerge convinced that you are not alone in your journey.

Let the healing begin.

....

CHAPTER 1

Trauma Responses and PTSD: Normal Reactions to Abnormal Events

Waking Him

Quietly she calls him
"Daddy . . . Daddy, are you sleeping?"
She has to begin the waking slowly,
if she is too sudden, he will uncoil
a fierce spring rusted loose.

Gently she must nudge him back
into the world of fenced-in yards
and refrigerator art, and away
from the shadowy echoes of rotten canvas and death.

She knows her child hand is not enough
because she is in some of those dreams,
staggering with him, shoeless through mud.
That is all he will say. He tries
to protect her from the terror, but she hears
the screams at night. She already knows.

She must use caution in the waking.

—JESSICA ORANGE

As I reread this poem our daughter wrote when she was still a teenager, I realize that she grasped the presence and shock wave effects of my husband's post-traumatic stress disorder (PTSD) before we knew enough to name it.

There is power in naming. For example, I have late-onset asthma. Prior to its diagnosis a few years ago, I was exhibiting symptoms that increasingly nipped away at my sense of self. I've always enjoyed hiking, but grew discouraged when I got winded on even short walks. Michael would patiently wait for me to catch my breath or firmly grasp my hand to help me up hills that only months before had been easy for me to climb. I felt old, out of shape, and horribly embarrassed that I could not keep up with my husband. We both valued our walks. They were special times to reconnect, slow down, and really be together, and I worried we might lose them.

When I finally saw my doctor, he ordered a pulmonary function test that I flunked. Yet I felt an almost happy relief when he said I had asthma. My doctor prescribed an inhaler and offered other guidance. I grew stronger, able to walk farther and more vigorously on each outing with Michael. We talked about how concerned Michael had been, and we were both buoyed by the knowledge that this was a problem that had a course of action. It could be treated. I would get better. There was power in the knowing, in the naming.

This is how we felt when Michael was finally diagnosed with PTSD in 2003. With that diagnosis came the realization that there were things we could do and experts we could each consult. We came to understand that so many of our actions and reactions over the course of our marriage were linked to trauma and PTSD. The pieces of the puzzle were coming together. We grew stronger and closer.

PTSD did not become an official diagnosis until 1980 when the American Psychiatric Association added it to its *Diagnostic and Statistical Manual of Mental Disorders,* but the effects of trauma on human beings are well documented throughout literature and history. In fact, Greek author and "father of history" Herodotus wrote of fifth-century B.C. warriors with PTSD symptoms. In his *A Short*

History of PTSD, Steve Bentley writes of how Herodotus describes an unwounded Athenian soldier who went blind after seeing his comrade get killed and how a Spartan was so shaken by battle he was nicknamed "the Trembler."

Shakespeare and Homer have described the effects of trauma, and post-traumatic stress symptoms are also described throughout U.S. military history. In Civil War times, PTSD was called *soldier's heart* or *Da Costa's Syndrome*, after Jacob Mendes Da Costa, the doctor who described an anxiety disorder with symptoms that mimicked heart disease. In World War I, doctors called it *shell shock*, or *combat fatigue*, and in World War II it was also known as *gross stress reaction*.

Because war and trauma go hand in hand, and we've probably had battles as long as we've had people on this earth, post-traumatic stress and PTSD symptoms are commonly linked to soldiers. But, as Bentley points out, there are also early accounts of trauma's after-effects among civilians such as Samuel Pepys, an Englishman who lived in London during the 1600s. Fortunately, Pepys kept a diary in which he entered his account of the Great Fire of London in 1666. Although his own house was saved, he describes his great fear, insomnia, and nightmares that persisted long after he witnessed the disaster.

Railway crashes were fairly common in the early nineteenth century, when the term *railway spine* was used to explain the post-traumatic symptoms of survivors of these accidents. Bentley describes how English author Charles Dickens told of his own horror at seeing the dead and dying when he was involved in a railway collision in 1865. "I am not quite right within," Dickens wrote in a letter after the event, and he remained "baffled" as to why his shaking and uneasiness grew worse, not less, as time passed.

The World War II term *gross stress reaction* actually made its way into the very first *Diagnostic and Statistical Manual of Mental Disorders (DSM-I)* created by the American Psychiatric Association in 1952. This diagnosis described acute psychological responses to those who had experienced problems from an extreme stressor (with no mention of any possible long-term effects). *Gross stress reaction* was dropped altogether in *DSM-II* in 1968, and mention of a stress-related anxiety disorder didn't reappear until 1980 in *DSM-III*, when *post-traumatic stress disorder* was first included.

We can thank our Vietnam veterans and those who worked with them for getting PTSD accepted as a legitimate and diagnosable medical condition with long-lasting effects for the millions of people who experience serious trauma. In the early 1970s, a group of psychiatrists used *post-Vietnam syndrome* to describe delayed reactions like the depression, anger, isolation, and sleeplessness they observed among these veterans. Their advocacy on behalf of these veterans led to *post-traumatic stress disorder* being entered into *DSM-III*.

Since 1980, the criteria for diagnosing PTSD have been argued over, tweaked, and expanded. The most recent diagnostic features appear in *DSM-IV* (2000), and might change again in *DSM-V,* due out sometime in 2012. PTSD expert Dr. Judith Lewis Herman of Harvard University says that an additional diagnosis called *complex PTSD* is needed to describe symptoms of long-term trauma, in which a person experiences repeated trauma over the course of months or years. Complex PTSD can result from situations such as prostitution brothels; long-term domestic violence; long-term, severe physical abuse; childhood sexual abuse; organized child exploitation rings; concentration camps; and prisoner-of-war camps.

The yardstick used to measure PTSD will probably never be perfect, but it is important for the medical and therapeutic communities, the Department of Veterans Affairs (VA), patients, and insurance companies to have a tool by which to measure symptoms and design appropriate treatment.

Shock Waves is not an academic text about trauma and PTSD. It is intended to help family and friends better understand what *they, and their loved one,* might be feeling and experiencing—whether or not the trauma survivor has had an official diagnosis of PTSD. If you have a friend or family member who has experienced severe trauma, this book will help you see how untended symptoms can spill over and affect you (or those closest to the trauma survivor) to the point where you also experience problems.

A PTSD Diagnosis

To be diagnosed with PTSD, *DSM-IV* specifies that a person must have been exposed to or have witnessed a traumatic event that involved actual or threatened death or serious injury to oneself or others. PTSD can also come from experiencing the unexpected or violent death, serious harm, or threat of harm, of someone close to you—family member or not.

> *I work in Manhattan, and when 9/11 happened my daughter was only five. For years she was terrified that when I went to work, I might not come home. She knew that I worked on the twenty-second floor of a much taller building, and she was afraid that a plane would hit the tall building I worked in, and I would not be able to get out. For the first year after that horrible event she had nightmares about people leaping out of burning buildings. It's been eight years. My daughter is thirteen now, and while she feels pretty confident that I will come home at night, she is still scared of being in really tall buildings.** *

In a PTSD diagnosis, the person's response to the trauma involves intense fear, helplessness, or horror. In children, the response might show up as disorganized or agitated behavior.

Duration and Intensity

To be classified as having PTSD, the traumatized person must have symptoms in three areas (reliving the trauma, avoidance and numbing,

---

*Indented text throughout this book represents the words of others: trauma survivors, those affected by a loved one's trauma or PTSD, and those who work with trauma survivors and their families. These persons are presented anonymously to protect the privacy of those involved, and in some cases, some details have been changed to ensure anonymity.

and hyperarousal) and these symptoms must last for more than one month.

Those diagnosed with PTSD have difficulty going about their daily tasks because their relationships, jobs, and often every aspect of their lives are significantly affected by their symptoms.

Reliving the Trauma

For people with PTSD, the traumatic event is reexperienced in one (or more) of the following ways:

- Recurrent or intrusive thoughts, images, or memories of the event. Young children may show signs of PTSD in their play, speech, or drawings.
- Nightmares or distressing dreams in which the trauma re-emerges. Children might have frightening dreams with no recognizable content.
- Flashbacks, illusions, or hallucinations. These images might cause the person to act or feel as if the traumatic event was still occurring, giving him or her a sense of re-living the experience.
- Mental or emotional anguish when something happens to trigger a recollection of some aspect of the event. For children abused by a family member, it could be seeing that uncle at a family reunion years after the abuse occurred. For those who have lived or worked in war-torn areas, a car backfiring may sound like an explosion or gunfire.
- Physical reactions when something triggers a memory of the trauma. For example, a person may react to a trigger with a stomach ache, a pounding heart or rapid breathing, sweating, or a severe headache.

Traumatic recollections might be triggered by an anniversary of the trauma; certain odors, sounds, textures, tastes, or sights; a medical procedure; an activity that replicates some aspect of the event; something that ignites fear like a close call on the freeway; certain places or spaces; a movie; a song; or by any event or stimulus.

Avoidance and Numbing

People with PTSD adopt certain strategies to avoid places, objects, or people that remind them of the traumatic event. In a person diagnosed with PTSD, three (or more) of the following need to be present:

- An effort to avoid thoughts, feelings, or conversations associated with the trauma
- An effort to avoid activities, places, or people that bring the trauma to mind
- An inability to remember an important aspect of the trauma
- A noticeable disinterest in doing things that were enjoyable before the traumatic experience (often called *psychic numbing* or *emotional anesthesia*)
- A feeling of detachment or estrangement from others
- Difficulty having or showing loving feelings or being intimate or sexual
- A sense of a foreshortened future in which the person doesn't expect to have a career, marriage, children, or a normal life span

Hyperarousal

People with PTSD are anxious or on the alert, making it difficult for them to relax. In a PTSD diagnosis, according to *DSM-IV*, two (or more) of the following symptoms are present:

- Difficulty falling or staying asleep (which could be due to nightmares about the trauma)
- Irritability or outbursts of anger
- Difficulty concentrating on or completing tasks

- Hypervigilance (which is an extreme sense of caution that may sometimes resemble paranoia)
- Exaggerated startle response

Acute, Chronic, and Delayed Onset PTSD

DSM-IV refers to three distinctions under the PTSD umbrella that specify onset and duration of the symptoms:

- **Acute PTSD** refers to symptoms that last less than three months;
- **Chronic PTSD** refers to symptoms that last three months or longer;
- **Delayed Onset PTSD** refers to symptoms that did not appear until after six months or more have passed between the traumatic event and the onset of symptoms.

....

WHAT'S IN A NAME?

Take a moment to review the diagnostic criteria for PTSD. Remember that it is *normal* to be upset after a trauma. It is *common* to have some of these PTSD symptoms after experiencing or witnessing a traumatic event. While it may be tempting to identify your loved one, yourself, or someone you know as having PTSD, leave the actual diagnosis up to a professional.

There is power—both positive and negative—in attaching a name to a cluster of symptoms. Having a diagnosis can be a relief to some people, but sometimes fear of being branded with PTSD keeps those who are deeply troubled in the aftermath of trauma from getting much-needed help. Many people with post-traumatic stress symptoms worry they might be seen as weak, crazy, or undependable by others if they ask for help; some think seeing a therapist could hurt their jobs.

Untreated post-traumatic symptoms (whether or not they turn out to be PTSD) can grow worse and negatively affect an entire family. Such symptoms can also be related to other treatable physical or mental health problems, so it is important to get guidance in sorting out what treatment is most appropriate.

Try not to get hung up attempting to figure out if someone's symptoms constitute PTSD, but do seek help if you sense your life might be spinning out of control.

And if there is a PTSD diagnosis, recognize that defining a disorder does not define the person. A person with cancer, for example, is not the disease. We are unique tapestries, made up of varied patterns and different threads. We are so much more than a title, an experience, an illness, or a diagnosis.

....

Normal Stress vs. Trauma

Life is filled with stressful times, but the moments usually pass and, with them, the stress. A frustrating home repair finally gets accomplished, or we break down and hire a plumber; a child passes an exam, or we hire a tutor; we make up with our partner after an argument; or a consistently crabby coworker at last apologizes. Some events, like births, a marriage, the natural death of an elderly parent, a new job, new house, or new town, can cause longer-lasting and greater stress, but they're still pretty common occurrences, not trauma. The child is born, the wedding takes place, the parent is mourned, the job gets more comfortable, the boxes get unpacked, and life goes on.

Stress performs an important function in our lives, and not all stress is bad. If a small child runs into the street, for example, our body's stress alarm system jolts us into action. Our heart rate speeds up and adrenaline pumps through us, allowing us to react quickly. We scoop up the child, plant her on safe ground, and breathe deeply once the danger has passed. This type of stress reaction is our body's way of protecting us by helping us stay focused and alert. The stress response can help us be sharper when we do things like negotiate with a boss, make a presentation, or communicate with a friend in a sticky situation.

Extreme or chronic stress is another matter. For caregivers and families of trauma survivors, constant stress is often an unwelcome visitor.

> *I was a mess for many years before my husband got help with his PTSD. I carried a lot of stress for the whole family, and my health was poor. My immune system became weak. After he completely broke down, I was a wreck. I cried when anyone asked me a personal question such as "how are you?" I was unable to reach out to others compassionately.*

When you live with a trauma survivor, you often live in a tension-filled environment where emotional abuse is not uncommon and the fear of physical abuse only adds to the extreme stress you are already feeling. Studies have shown that men and women who experienced the trauma of physical abuse, sexual abuse, or emotional neglect as children may be more likely to be abusive in intimate adult relationships than those who did not have these experiences. The victims of this ongoing domestic abuse (both emotional or physical) can also develop post-traumatic symptoms.

Symptoms of chronic stress like tension headaches, fatigue, and irritability become so familiar, they often go unchecked. But these symptoms are related to that same instinctive response that causes us to rescue a child from danger. They are our body's way of telling us that we need to take notice. In the case of rescuing a child, that alert prompted us to move quickly. In the case of stress symptoms, we're being alerted to pull back and slow down, if even for a moment. Prolonged or excessive stress can lead to medical problems and depression.

You might say that *normal* stress is a bump in the road of life that you navigate over or around with minor difficulty. Trauma, however, is like a California highway after an earthquake—the road suddenly opens up, you lose control, and you slide in, terrified. The damages sustained will vary from person to person.

Different people have different trauma thresholds, just as they have different pain thresholds. While some people exposed to traumatic events do not develop PTSD, others go on to develop the full-blown syndrome. What's important to keep in mind is that it is absolutely appropriate to react to trauma with powerful emotions. In "Disaster and Your Mental Health," the National Mental Health Association (NMHA) pointed out that after 9/11, "for most people, the intense feelings of anxiety, sadness, grief, and anger have been healthy and appropriate."

Here are some common reactions to trauma that the NMHA compiled:

- Disbelief and shock
- Fear and anxiety about the future
- Disorientation; difficulty making decisions or concentrating
- Inability to focus
- Apathy and emotional numbing
- Irritability and anger
- Sadness and depression
- Feeling powerless
- Extreme changes in eating patterns; loss of appetite or overeating
- Crying for "no apparent reason"
- Headaches or stomach problems
- Difficulty sleeping
- Excessive use of alcohol and [other] drugs

Notice how almost all of the above *common* responses to trauma show up in the *DSM-IV* criteria for PTSD. Remember, it is the *intensity and duration of reactions and feelings* that distinguish common reactions to trauma from PTSD. Think of it this way: Two people are exposed to the same germs in the same setting, and both end up getting colds.

One is miserable for a week or so, but recovers completely. Symptoms grow worse for the other person, however, and progress into serious pneumonia. Trauma can affect anyone, young or old, rich or poor. The more disturbing the trauma, the greater the risk for PTSD.

Reacting to trauma and even having PTSD does not mean we're weird or crazy; it means we're human beings with the capacity to feel deeply. That's not a bad thing.

What Do PTSD Symptoms Look Like in "Real Life"?

Sleep disturbances not only affect the trauma survivor, they can also interfere with the sleep of partners and children. As Jessica's poem so poignantly reveals, she learned early on to "begin the waking slowly" and not startle her dad by poking him or calling to him too loudly if he was sleeping. The dreams aren't as frequent now, but Michael (like so many others with PTSD) still has occasional nightmares.

Survivors of sexual abuse, for example, may carry such powerful body memories that they see their molester in dream after dream— even though the abuse occurred decades before, in their childhood. Some trauma survivors so dread these nightmares that they medicate themselves with alcohol or other drugs in an effort to numb themselves to sleep. Others may fight sleep altogether and suffer the physical maladies that accompany insomnia.

> *Nights bring it all back to me, because that's when my stepfather would sneak into my room when I was just a little girl. When I do sleep, I usually sleep so lightly that I awake suddenly, startled by any creak, any footstep. My jumpiness, of course, wakes my partner, then we're both crabby the next day because of lack of sleep. If I do manage to sleep deeply, my nightmares are so vivid that my whole body tenses to ward off the dream attacker and I awake sore, with clenched fists.*

I thought I was used to the nightmares, but just recently, Michael leaped to the foot of the bed and yelled for me to "take cover" because he imagined he heard a mortar round go off. Although a fairly common part of the post-traumatic landscape, such dreams can be frightening to trauma survivors and those who love them.

> *I was the victim of random violence, and my mind just could not stop trying to process the experience. Each dream always had me trying to avoid getting shot, being trapped, and getting absolutely blown away. Think violent video game, only worse. The nightmares continued on and off for years. The first year was horrible. There were times when I would wake up during the night on the floor next to my bed, thinking the attacker was coming down the hallway toward my second floor bedroom. I remember having processed my options for escape. More than once, I had to talk myself down from just jumping out of my window and falling to the cement patio fifteen feet below. . . . [If it weren't] for therapy teaching me skills to find reason in the midst of these dream hallucination sequences, I'd have jumped. There were many times when I hadn't slept, was exhausted, and feared sleeping, that I wished it would just be over. I wanted to die to be free of the terror.*

Sometimes, family members not involved in the actual catastrophic event are nonetheless bothered by intrusive dreams and images of what they imagine their loved ones suffered:

> *For the past two years, I have had recurrent nightmares of the airplane crash that killed my husband and our close friend. I was supposed to be his copilot that day. . . . In the dream, I'm flying in the air behind the plane and I try to tell him to abort the landing, to get out of there, to save themselves. Consciously, I know he's gone and will never be coming home, but emotionally, I was not ready to let him go.*

I knew about nightmares after trauma, but I had never heard of "daymares" until a friend of ours with PTSD described how disturbing it was to walk down a street in broad daylight and feel certain he saw a stranger's head in front of him explode, which was one of the images burned into his brain from his trauma. Since his revelation, I've heard of others who struggle with daytime hallucinations.

What made it really hard was the dreams converted immediately into hallucinations. Even as I tried to wake myself out of dreams, they became embedded in my waking reality. I couldn't tell when I was awake or asleep; what was real or imagined. It all blurred.

Often, something—a sight, smell, sound, or texture—will send someone back to the traumatic event.

Dealing with the [body] remains was the main source of my PTSD, and these experiences have a life of their own even to this day. For me, the remains are connected as a constant daily reminder to things like airports, aircraft noise, the smell of gasoline and jet fuel, funerals, and aluminum in any form or shape. These things have the same power to evoke disturbing memories, run the tape loop in my head, of the death and destruction in Vietnam. It's crazy! I just put plastic handles on the drawers and vanity in my bathroom. I hate the plastic ones, but every time I use the brushed aluminum ones, I remember the coffins.

Adaptive Behaviors

Now that our family has learned more about PTSD, we understand that some of Michael's symptoms were adaptive behaviors that kept him alive in Vietnam. He said one of the best pieces of advice he got in his first days in combat came from a more experienced soldier who told him to "leave the world behind." Vietnam, he said, was the only reality, and those other things were distractions that could get you killed. "He was right," said Michael. "While I was there, I didn't have a past or a future. All I had—all I could have—was 'war time.'"

Many rape and trauma victims also describe numbing and detachment (shutting down or feeling "outside" of one's body) as adaptive strategies during their trauma.

> *Shutting down after the first rape was easy. I was only thirteen and my family was acting weird, like they had all been attacked, so I didn't feel welcome to share my fears. Too, the police never pursued a suspect. I confronted the city judge about it, and he told me I wouldn't be able to pick him out in a lineup because they would all look alike and be dressed alike. So I buried everything inside.*

Difficulties arise when trauma survivors "reenter" the world and find that, months later, they are still numb.

> *I have learned that if you suppress your feelings, as I did for decades, your feelings will eventually bite you in the ass before you know what hit you. I have had two nervous breakdowns, but I am learning who I am and how the sexual traumas in my life have affected me, and I'm learning that it's okay to feel the way I do as long as I acknowledge my feelings, identify where they are coming from, and face them head-on. In other words, I'm living through hell right now.*

Many withdraw or isolate themselves. Others describe "going through the motions" of living, blocking out the past, and not daring to think about the future.

> *I remember the wives of firemen saying that their husbands went to work that day on 9/11, and it was like an alien took over their bodies and came home in their place.*

Hypervigilance

Hypervigilance is another survival skill that serves survivors well under certain circumstances. First responders, soldiers, and women who find themselves in threatening situations, for example, learn to quickly scan their surroundings for potential dangers—actions that can keep them and others safe. For many trauma survivors, being alert becomes instinctive and natural, and they are able to relax once they have assessed a situation and figured out an escape if an emergency were to arise.

When caution grows into extreme (and long-lasting) hypervigilance, however, it is a post-traumatic symptom that can interfere with day-to-day life.

> *The most lasting impact of the shooting is hypervigilance. For years I didn't go anywhere without instantly, subconsciously, and sometimes consciously mapping out escape routes. Any room, any home, any meeting place. I knew windows, doors, hallways to get out. I mapped distances I could leap from a window to safety. I always kept my back to a wall. I'd go to meetings and have to use every therapy trick in the book to not freak out that an angry person was going to pull a gun and trap me in the room. When you are running calming exercises in your head, it's hard to hear the questions being asked. I developed two parallel minds: one that was present to reality and one that was present to my fear. People probably didn't notice me clutching a little marble in my left hand to work out the fear mind while my right hand held the marker to write on the flip charts. Literally, a tool in each hand . . . [one for each mind].*

How a Loved One's Symptoms Can Affect Others

I remember so clearly the day my therapist asked, "Who is helping you with *your* war?" I wept in gratitude that someone was at last connecting the dots and helping me understand there was something more going on in our household than "she's demanding; he's distant."

For so many years, I took responsibility for our family's emotional well-being. I couldn't sort out what things were my responsibilities, what things were Michael's, and what things needed joint attention. Michael often dodged getting in touch with his feelings by escaping into workaholism or compulsive exercise. He was a perfectionist, and he attacked house projects with the same compulsion. If I tried to help with yard work or projects, he would often go back over what I had done, bringing it up to his standards. Although he took care not to openly criticize the way I kept house, I sensed his disapproval and badgered him to tell me what he was feeling. Unable to identify his feelings, he'd walk away and I'd get angry or depressed, feeling rejected and unloved. We got very good at our respective dysfunctional behaviors. I often felt like an inadequate partner and a whiner. What right did I have to complain about a good father and hardworking husband?

I worried about his nightmares, and wondered about his insatiable need to see every movie about Vietnam. The war stories he told me early in our marriage were seared in my mind, but he filed them away deep within himself and buried the photographs from Vietnam he had shown me deep in the attic. He didn't talk about Vietnam until Jessica was in eighth grade. Her social studies teacher asked if any of his students' parents had served in the war, and Jessica told him that her dad had. Michael agreed to come in and talk to Jessica's class, and he struggled to get through his presentation. When the inevitable "Did you kill anybody?" question came, he tried, unsuccessfully, to give the honest answer, "It was my job to kill people," through his tears. He came home distraught and sullen, and Jessica came home looking frightened and confused.

Still, we didn't see the link between his trauma and our problems. We partied hard with friends and played hard with Jessica. We got very good at ignoring our problems (if you don't count my therapy for depression, Michael's workaholism, or our couples' communication class). If anyone asked how we were doing, we'd say "great," and usually believed it. And when I asked Michael how he was, he often replied, "It's a good day, nobody's shooting at me." What's that line about denial not just being a river in Egypt?

As we discovered, a loved one's trauma can affect families in many ways. Without warning or intention, individuals with PTSD symptoms often experience intrusive memories or dreams that are so vivid they reexperience the initial trauma and react with grief, guilt, fear, or anger.

For many, many years now, I get rambunctious at night. It got so bad, I was bruising my wife so often, that we've had to sleep in separate rooms ever since. It helps to sleep with a light on because I used to wake up in the middle of a nightmare where there's an attacker after me, and turning on the light made him disappear. Even though I have been going to both group and individual therapy, I still lash out a lot during my nightmares. Three years ago, I was sleeping in the lower bunk bed in my son's fishing camp, and I punched the upper bunk rail so hard I broke the ring finger of my right hand.

Although anger can be a natural—even healthy—emotion, it can also have unhealthy expressions that lead to marital, relationship, or family difficulties; job problems; and loss of friendships.

My son with PTSD has anger issues. He has dreams and sleep issues, so he takes sleeping pills. He drinks excessively and fights when he is drinking. At a family wedding, my son wanted to go to the pool and had an argument with the [hotel's] night manager. They eventually called the police and called us down from our room. Once, he fell asleep when he was in the shower. My older son called us at 2:00 in the morning because he didn't know if he was dead or alive. When he isn't drinking, he's a wonderful, loving kid, and we all enjoy him. His brothers and sisters aren't that patient. They feel we should let him deal with his own problems and not interfere. They think if he messes up and goes to jail, he may finally realize he has a problem.

Children, especially, can be frightened by these symptoms and start to worry about their parent's well-being or their own safety.

I remember the night he flew into a rage about something that was inconsequential. The kids were pretty little then. He threw a chair across the dining room and broke it. He cried and begged me for forgiveness, but I was frozen and couldn't respond with compassion.

Those with PTSD may also avoid places or experiences that could trigger memories. They may avoid going to the store, the movies, or restaurants, or doing things that were enjoyable for the family before the onset of PTSD. Sufferers become numb to feelings and withdraw from interpersonal interactions, except perhaps with those who have been there, such as other veterans or other survivors of an accident or disaster. This isolation can leave loved ones feeling rejected, lonely, and confused.

I was eight months pregnant when the Pentagon got hit on 9/11. My husband got out, in shock, but he lost twenty-eight of his friends. Our baby was born [soon after], but got very sick, and we were in the process of moving. My husband had no chance to grieve. Then he was sent to Iraq. I think he was already dealing with PTSD issues from 9/11, which got worse from Iraq. He wasn't sleeping and became very isolated. He didn't want anything to do with me or the family. He shut down and became very indifferent. I was lonely, whether or not he was here. I remember telling him, "You're here, but not here. Your body is here, but your mind is elsewhere. You're like a robot."

Hyperarousal shows up as difficulty sleeping, impaired concentration, being easily startled or highly irritated, or acting unduly concerned for personal safety and the safety of loved ones. These symptoms can be easily misinterpreted as hostility or distancing, causing children, spouses, and loved ones to feel uncared for, frightened, and insecure.

A minister molested my wife when she was only twelve, and she can't stand to be touched unexpectedly as a result of that trauma.

The kids and I know not to give her spontaneous hugs or shake her shoulder to wake her up, but sometimes friends or family forget and reach out to her in a gesture of affection. She gets this frightened look in her eyes when that happens and just goes stiff or seems ready to bolt. It took us a long time and a lot of therapy before she could relax enough to be sexually intimate, but things are much better now than they used to be.

Work can also be a challenge for some people with PTSD because they feel inadequate, anxious, overwhelmed, or depressed, or they may have trouble concentrating. Resultant money issues can add to stress at home, causing arguments and fear. Men and women with PTSD may also dive into a job and work obsessively to avoid thinking or feeling the effects of trauma.

After the war, I wanted to have sleep patterns like normal people, but that didn't work for me. I'd work until I was physically and mentally exhausted and then I'd finally fall asleep by one or two in the morning and then sleep to five or six a.m. I'd work long hours or if I wasn't working, I'd do something else, fifty to sixty hours a week. I might go to bed but I'd either not sleep or only sleep for an hour and then I'd wake up thinking about Vietnam and go for a ride on my bike or something else to escape the thoughts.

Attempted and Completed Suicide
Perhaps the most tragic consequences of PTSD are attempted and completed suicides. This woman survived war and rape, and, thankfully, lived to tell the story of how close she came to killing herself. Her account reminded me of the Kirk Douglas story, only in her case it was her cats, not a bad tooth, that saved her.

I loaded my .357 magnum (the one I slept with every night) with hollow-point bullets so it would blow off half of my head, then I spun the cylinder and cocked the hammer. I was ready to fire, when my two cats came running in and jarred me back to reality. I took my finger off the trigger, uncocked the hammer, lowered the gun, and took out the bullets. Then I put the gun away and picked up my cats.

Some stories, however, don't end as well.

Kevin and Joyce Lucey sign their emails with their names, adding, the line: "The proud parents of Cpl. Jeffrey Michael Lucey, a 23-year-old USMC reservist forever. Succumbed to the hidden wounds of PTSD on 06/22/04." I use their real names here because they have been very public about their son's suicide. When Jeff returned from Iraq, Joyce said they watched him fall apart. He had panic attacks, trouble sleeping, nightmares, and poor appetite, and he was isolating himself in his room. He was depressed and drinking. When his dad called the local Veterans Affairs office to describe what was happening, they said it was classic PTSD and said Jeff should come in as soon as possible. He was admitted for four days, and during that time he told the VA about the three methods of suicide he had thought about—overdose, suffocation, and hanging. This was not relayed to his parents, however, and he was released June 1, 2004, with the VA telling them Jeff couldn't be assessed for PTSD until he was alcohol free.

Jeff got worse, and his parents tried to get him help, but received no guidance on how to handle the situation. Like many worried family members, they became as hypervigilant as trauma survivors. They hid knives and took away anything they thought Jeff might use to harm himself, even disabling his car. Civilian authorities said they couldn't help either, because Jeff was drinking. On June 21, Kevin described Jeff as being in a total rage. This time Kevin called the Vet Center and said the "angel" who answered calmed both Jeff and Kevin down. Just before midnight, Kevin said Jeff asked him for the second time in ten days if he could sit on his dad's lap and rock him like he used to when Jeff was little.

At the March 2008 Winter Soldier hearings where veterans of the Iraq and Afghanistan wars gave accounts of their experiences,

Kevin Lucey ended his testimony by saying, "The next day I came home. It was about 7:15. I held Jeff one last time as I lowered his body from the rafters and took the hose from around his neck . . ." Here's what they said when I asked Kevin and Joyce how they dealt with Jeff's suicide:

> *Each family has to handle it in their own way, but it never crossed our minds not to be open. We felt it was a tragic way to die, but a tragedy would have been further promoted if we had lied about how he had died. At his wake, we just put it out there. Some of his unit was there, and we begged them not to do as Jeff did—we knew the officers were concerned about two other men. . . . We met one of the officers six months later and he told us that both of them came up and said they needed help.*
>
> *We've gotten lots of calls from distraught families who are worried about their sons and daughters. There was a family about thirty miles from us who saw our story on television and called us for help. Their son's name was also Jeffrey Michael, just like our son. We referred them to the right people and got a note about three months ago, saying "your Jeffrey saved our Jeffrey." We don't want others to go through what we did. People need to know that PTSD can be lethal.*

These stories are not meant to scare or depress you, and you may never have to deal with the threat or reality of suicide. However, it is important to know, as Kevin Lucey put it so well, "PTSD can be lethal"—as can other post-trauma behaviors like depression or alcohol and other drug abuse. Although women attempt suicide more often than men, men are more likely to succeed in killing themselves during a suicide attempt. Research shows that among people who have had a diagnosis of PTSD at some point in their lifetime, approximately 27 percent have also attempted suicide.

When traumatized loved ones are in such despair that they are in danger of hurting or killing themselves, their family and friends can become overwhelmed with worry or paralyzed by their feelings of fear and helplessness. Any sense of normalcy a family may have enjoyed before these trauma symptoms appeared often vanishes as more and more attention is focused on the traumatized loved one. Many concerned family and friends become hypervigilant in their efforts to keep their loved one safe, as the Luceys did with Jeff.

Kevin and Joyce Lucey would give anything to have their son back, and they mourn his death every day. But they emphasize that as much as they miss him, they have learned that his suicide was not their fault. While they will always carry a burden of loss, they do not carry the additional burden of guilt. Ultimately, "to be or not to be" is an individual and independent choice. We can support, try to help, and try to understand our loved ones, but we cannot control their lives *or* their deaths. We cannot fix them; we can only love them unconditionally, and we can take care of ourselves as we experience the shock wave effects of our loved one's trauma.

We can also be grateful for the families who tell the truth about their loved one's suicide, because the stories just might cause a trauma survivor or family member to get the help she or he needs. In this way, the voices of those lost to us by suicide are still heard.

Warning Signs for Suicide
Seek help as soon as possible by contacting a mental health professional or by calling the National Suicide Prevention Lifeline at 1-800-273-TALK (see sidebar) if you or someone you know exhibits any of the following signs:

- Threatening to hurt or kill oneself or talking about wanting to hurt or kill oneself
- Looking for ways to kill oneself by seeking access to firearms or medications, or by other means
- Talking or writing about death, dying, or suicide when these actions are out of the ordinary for the person
- Feeling hopeless

- Feeling rage or uncontrolled anger or seeking revenge
- Acting reckless or engaging in risky activities, seemingly without thinking
- Feeling trapped—like there's no way out
- Increasing alcohol or other drug use
- Withdrawing from friends, family, and society
- Feeling anxious, agitated, or unable to sleep or sleeping all the time
- Experiencing dramatic mood changes
- Seeing no reason for living or having no sense of purpose in life

....

CALL 1-800-273-TALK (1-800-273-8255) IF YOU OR A LOVED ONE IS IN CRISIS

Call the National Suicide Prevention Lifeline at 1-800-273-TALK (8255) if you are feeling desperate, alone, or hopeless. It is a free, twenty-four-hour hotline available to anyone in suicidal crisis or emotional distress. Your call will be routed to your nearest crisis center. The hotline is staffed around the clock by trained counselors, and this service is free and confidential. In addition to helping you on the phone, counselors can provide information about mental health services in your area. More information can be found on the National Suicide Prevention Lifeline's Web site at www.suicidepreventionlifeline.org.

Who should call?
- Anyone who feels sad, hopeless, or suicidal
- Family and friends who are concerned about a loved one
- Anyone interested in mental health treatment and service referrals

Why should you call?
The Lifeline Network answers thousands of calls from people

in emotional distress. There are many reasons for their calls. Please call for any of the following reasons:

- Suicidal thoughts
- Information on suicide
- Information on mental health
- Substance abuse or addiction
- To help a friend or loved one
- Relationship problems
- Abuse or violence
- Economic problems
- Sexual orientation issues
- Physical illness
- Loneliness
- Family problems

....

Healing from Trauma Is a Family Affair

Family members hang in delicate balance, connected at the center like a wind chime. If something—good or bad—tugs at one member, the others may lose their equilibrium and come clanging together noisily. This reaction is especially true for families who have loved ones struggling in the aftermath of a traumatic event. People who shared their stories in this chapter describe how a loved one shut down, withdrew, or seemed like an alien or robot. Family and friends are often left feeling confused, angry, sad, worried, or lonely when the loved one they knew so well changes in the wake of trauma.

The Greek poet Agathon wrote, "Even god cannot change the past." As much as we'd like to erase a loved one's trauma, we cannot, any more than we can spare them or control the hard work of their healing, which often means they are learning to feel again. But we can educate ourselves about trauma and its effects and take good care of ourselves as we stand beside them while they heal.

When you familiarize yourself with the common reactions to trauma and the symptoms of PTSD, you change the lens through which you see the world. When Michael and I first saw the 1993 movie *Fearless,* he hadn't yet been diagnosed with PTSD, but we were strangely drawn to this film and the ways in which Jeff Bridges' character changed dramatically after he survived a plane crash in which his business partner was killed. In fact, we were so moved by the film that we immediately bought it for ourselves. When we watched it again after we understood more about PTSD and trauma, we cried together at the story's poignancy and the mirror it was for the millions like us who have been affected by trauma. It's not that we now see PTSD symptoms around every corner; it's that we have a heightened awareness and tenderness for ourselves and others.

Knowledge led us to action, and action led us to healing and a fuller sense of happiness. There's freedom in that realization. As Miriam Greenspan writes in her book *Healing through the Dark Emotions:*

> For those who desperately need a way to feel more hopeful, resilient, and joyful, take heart! The emotions that appear to afflict us can be the vehicles of our liberation from suffering. Experiencing our grief, fear, and despair in a new light, we renew our capacities for gratitude, joy, and faith. We grow in courage and compassion. We approach the world with less fear and more wonder. We have more energy for changing the things that matter. These gifts can only be found when we are unafraid to dance the dance of dark emotions in our lives.
>
> Let's dance.

....

THE SERENITY PRAYER

There are several versions of the *Serenity Prayer,* so enthusiastically embraced by Alcoholics Anonymous (AA) when it was discovered in 1948. It has been variously attributed to an ancient Sanskrit text, to Aristotle, to St. Augustine, St. Francis of Assisi, and others. AA generally credits this version to theologian Reinhold Niebuhr:

God, grant me the serenity
To accept the things I cannot change,
Courage to change the things I can,
And wisdom to know the difference.

You don't have to be religious to recite this prayer; you don't even have to believe in a god. This simple twenty-five-word statement is a good reminder, however, that *we* aren't god. We can't control the fact that our loved one experienced a deep trauma, and we can't control our loved one's responses to that experience. However, we can ask for guidance and muster the courage it takes to change our own thinking and actions. We can arm ourselves with knowledge about trauma and its effects, and we can replenish our own reserves so we will stay healthy and so we will have the patience it takes for our loved one and our family to heal.

....

....

CHAPTER 2

Acknowledging Loss and Honoring Grief

> Grief, like despair, is an emotion that asks us to depart from the 'normal'—to be still, like a pool of frozen water in the winter. From out of this apparent stillness, an imperceptible movement occurs, from sorrow for what has been lost to gratitude for what remains. The trick is to let go and descend into grief's cold waters.
>
> —MIRIAM GREENSPAN,
> *Healing through the Dark Emotions*

SO MUCH ABOUT SURVIVING TRAUMA and loving a trauma survivor has to do with loss and grief. As Don R. Catherall, Ph.D., writes in his book *Back from the Brink: A Family Guide to Overcoming Traumatic Stress,* "Traumatization always involves some kind of loss—at the very least, a loss of beliefs (such as an illusion of security), attitudes (such as trust), meaning, and feelings of control. More often, there's a loss of dreams, of innocence, and of the basic sense of self. And sometimes, there are losses of actual people and physical abilities. The main problem with failing to acknowledge loss is that it interferes with the process of adapting, changing, and creating new avenues of fulfillment to replace the ones that are lost."

Read Catherall's words once more and sit with them for a moment. He writes, "**Traumatization always involves some kind of loss.**" If we are a spouse, child, parent, or close friend of a trauma survivor, we might be able to grasp what our loved one has lost as a result of a trauma, but too often we fail to recognize what *we ourselves* have lost in the wake of our loved one's trauma.

Our family first visited the Vietnam Memorial in Washington D.C. when Jessica was in high school. It struck me as a large, dark wing of death. It is carved into the earth, and you walk down a gradual slope to read the names of dead soldiers, etched into the smooth granite in the order in which they died. Jessica and I stood more than fifty feet from each other at each end of 1969–1970 (Michael's tour of duty), and I was taken aback by the enormity of the loss as I ran my fingers over the grooved letters that formed names.

These losses are tragic, but they are tangible, even touchable when you have a memorial, a cemetery marker, or an urn. Physical deaths can be mourned through ritual and in community, and the grief of those who mourn runs deep as family and friends gather to shed tears and memorialize their lost loved one. But Michael and millions of other trauma survivors did not die. He stood physically whole to photograph his wife and daughter at the Wall. He lived to trace the names of his fallen brothers. Our little family was still complete, while other families would never again see their loved one. The man I loved was still at my side. That reality is cause for celebration, not grief. What right did I have to feel loss?

A man who was very involved in erecting the outdoor memorial and the museum at the site of the Oklahoma City bombing told me of the opposition his group faced when deciding to list survivors as well as the dead.

We didn't want to "memorialize" survivors, but we wanted to make sure they were remembered. It took us eight months just to define "survivor" for the mission statement, and it was a difficult and often overwhelming process. Some who had lost loved ones were very opposed to the idea of a "survivors'" wall, telling us, "They're here. They survived, so why do they need to be acknowledged?" I don't think a survivors' wall had been done before, but it became an important part of the memorial and museum. We've also urged those involved in the 9/11 memorial in New York to do the same.

The planners of the Oklahoma City memorial held their ground, and the result is a stunning place of hope and healing. On the grounds where the Alfred P. Murrah Federal Building once stood are 168 bronze and stone chairs, each symbolizing a life lost, with smaller chairs to represent the 19 children killed in the blast. To the east are the only remaining walls from the Murrah Building, and they were left standing as a reminder of those who survived the terrorist attack, many with serious injuries. More than 600 names of these survivors are inscribed on salvaged pieces of granite from the former lobby.

I've visited this memorial twice, and I find it to be one of the most meaningful monuments I've ever visited—and the only one I've seen that takes into account how widespread the effects of trauma can be. The words at the memorial are inclusive, and as I read them, I felt as though they were written for me and for everyone else who had been touched by trauma, *any* trauma: "We come here to remember those who were killed, those who survived, and those changed forever. May all who leave here know the impact of violence. May this Memorial offer comfort, strength, peace, hope and serenity."

As these words underscore, trauma does change us forever, all of us—survivors, families, rescue workers, and healers. We will never be the same. This doesn't mean we won't grow stronger and healthier, or that our lives can't be richer and fuller than before the trauma. But our lives are changed, and it is important to grieve what we've lost before we can move forward into wholeness and healing.

It is understandable that trauma survivors suffer losses. Although they may not acknowledge it, it is also normal for other family members to experience loss when they give up pieces of themselves and their lives in an effort to support their traumatized loved one and hold the family together. It took many years (and many therapy sessions) for me to understand that I had a need—and a right—to grieve what I have lost. Being given permission to grieve was a gift that helped me cope with, then emerge from, the intermittent yet chronic depression I tried to ignore for such a long time.

Grief is a messy process, and despite all the books and discussions about "stages," it is usually a nonlinear process in which feelings can wash over you long after the trauma has passed. Hurricane Katrina struck in 2005, for example, but many Louisiana and Mississippi residents are still trying to pick up the pieces of their lives. Homes, livelihoods, and lives were lost, along with a sense of safety and security. Houses, businesses, and lives are being rebuilt, but those losses are still mourned.

Grieving Lost Innocence

When people talk about the effects of trauma and PTSD, they often describe a loss of innocence. The world doesn't seem as safe or predictable, and many emerge from a traumatic experience with more fear and anxiety—emotions that can have a long-lasting effect on other family members, as this child of Holocaust survivors recounts:

> *I have always felt that human beings were capable of terrible things and were being kept in check by tenuous bonds. That has made life fearful and I struggle with anxiety.*

I felt a loss of my own innocence early in our marriage one night after we had tucked Jessica into bed, when Michael said he was ready to have a "Vietnam night." He explained he just wanted to get it out of the way so he could be done with it. (If only it were that easy.) He spread his pictures from Vietnam out on the desk in the little trailer home we rented in Kent, Ohio. He matter-of-factly told me things he had told no one before that time, reciting horrors detachedly, as if they had happened to someone else. (I didn't know about emotional numbing back then).

I listened to his stories deep into that night and began to ache from the weight of that terrible war. Of course, I couldn't know what it was like to actually be there, but his descriptions of burning villages made my eyes sting. I imagined the villagers hugging themselves tight in fear and grief, as I drew a blanket tightly around me. I still remember the name of the little cat—Titi Lau—that was eaten by the rats. As he talked, I felt like I walked in jungle heat with him. Through his eyes, I saw two little boys get ripped apart by machine guns after they set off a homemade bomb that killed Michael's fellow marines.

Michael put the photographs back into their envelope, stuffing them and the memories away in his sea bag, and we didn't talk about these things until years later. But the stories and images stayed with me and even invaded my dreams on occasion. I was glad Michael trusted me enough to tell me his war stories, but in gaining his confidence I also lost something that night. The world seemed more fragile, less certain; a darker place where little boys and nineteen-year-olds could be made to kill and be killed. I grew more protective of Jessica, and more fearful for myself and those I loved.

A certain loss of idealism often accompanies a loss of innocence when trauma suddenly invades our once-secure world.

I was headed to a friend's house for a barbeque. It's a tree-lined neighborhood in the city. People were out on their porches, kids playing in the street. I'd been there many times and always felt safe; the 'tough' neighborhood was blocks away. I stepped out of the car, reached back in to grab the groceries, when three shots rang out. Pop, pop . . . pop. I can still hear the cadence. I don't remember those three to five seconds. I do remember yelling for help. As I tried to run, I felt my left leg going out and I hopped to the light pole, grabbed it and sat down, still yelling for help. Me, the good

*boy who never did drugs, spent my career serving poor people, vol-
unteering as a church youth director: I had been shot in a random
drive-by shooting.*

Witnessing, hearing about, or experiencing trauma shakes us
awake and makes us achingly aware of our vulnerability. Studies show
how children can exhibit post-traumatic symptoms from just seeing
or hearing news reports after a terrorist attack, a natural disaster, a
murder, or other catastrophe—not to mention all the kids who are
exposed to daily violence in their neighborhoods and homes. When
trauma strikes someone close, a piece of their childhood is lost, and
that initial loss makes them more susceptible to later traumas.

*I worry about my five-year-old niece. Her mother's sister died
of a rare illness when she was a little girl, so both the mom and
grandmother live in constant fear that my niece will contract the
same disease. They talk about the girl who died a lot, and any-
time my niece is sick—even with a little cold—they both hover
and noticeably worry. It's so obvious that my niece picks up on
their anxiety because she gets withdrawn and anxious or acts out
in some way. They've all become nervous wrecks, and sometimes
I just want to say, "Just let her be a normal kid!" But I can't. It's
really sad to see how trauma is "infecting" three generations.*

Grieving a Changed Relationship

Trauma survivors and their families learn the hard way that "happily ever after" is a simplistic notion best saved for greeting cards.
Happiness and family togetherness take hard work in the best of
circumstances. When unexpected trauma strikes a loved one, strong
bonds are tested and behaviors change in an effort to adapt to what
one wife of a trauma survivor described as her family's "new normal." The physical and emotional intimacy that both partners enjoyed before the effects of trauma materialized is often damaged or

diminished when symptoms grow stronger and more intrusive. We try to be patient and understanding, but we often miss our loved one during "trauma times," when a symptom is triggered or he or she withdraws in anger or silence into the darkness that trauma memories hold. This loss of intimacy is especially difficult for survivors of rape and sexual abuse and for those who love them.

Effects from such trauma might be present immediately afterwards or may not show up until long after the assault or abuse. Survivors of sexual abuse might become afraid of sex or approach sexual intercourse as an obligation. Traumatic thoughts or memories could be triggered by physical touch, which can be frightening for both partners. Male rape survivors might have difficulty getting an erection, and women might experience vaginal pain or trouble having an orgasm. Although these symptoms are normal and understandable and usually pass with time, they can be confusing and disturbing for a couple who longs for but cannot achieve the intimacy they once enjoyed.

In her book *Telling: A Memoir of Rape and Recovery*, Patricia Weaver Francisco recalls:

> My anger had already contributed to a growing distance in my marriage. When I withdrew sexually, Tim was faced with a strain of guilt by association. Was he somehow accountable for the sins of his gender? How could we engage while I was so withdrawn unless he initiated the seduction? Was that pressure? What is the relationship between erotic aggression and rape? Had the line moved? Would he overstep? He became trapped in one of those undecodable logical fallacies: *A man harmed the woman I love. I am a man. Therefore, I. . . .*
>
> When Tim inquired at various agencies about a support group for male partners, he was rebuffed. 'We don't have enough funding to take care of the *women* who need us,' scoffed one overburdened voice on the phone. *Give me a*

break, people in the field seemed to be saying—a rape support group for *men?*

There's greater recognition now for the fact that partners need help when their world has collapsed. The skills it takes to manage the strain that trauma places on a relationship are not common knowledge. This is another consequence of the silence we keep. Blindsided, we become statistics. *Eighty percent of marriages don't survive a rape.*

If your loved one is a survivor of rape or sexual abuse, it is important that you get appropriate help and work together to rebuild intimacy. It is crucial that your loved one feels safe and can trust that his or her limits will be respected.

....

CONTACT RAINN IF YOU OR A LOVED ONE HAS BEEN SEXUALLY ASSAULTED OR ABUSED

RAINN (Rape, Abuse, and Incest Network) is the nation's largest organization offering help to victims of sexual assault. It provides information for rape and incest victims, the media, policymakers, and other concerned individuals.

Among its many programs, RAINN also operates a National Sexual Assault Hotline at 1-800-656-HOPE (1-800-656-4673, Ext. 1), which is a partnership of more than 1,100 local rape treatment hotlines. This network provides free, confidential services around the clock. Since it began in 1994, the hotline has helped more than one million sexual assault victims.

In 2007, RAINN expanded its hotline services with the nation's first secure Online Hotline (www.rainn.org/get-help/national-sexual-assault-online-hotline). Specially trained crisis counselors offer free, anonymous, and completely confidential help twenty-four hours a day. In addition, the Online Hotline Web site provides a library of information about recovery, medical issues, the criminal justice process, local resources, and support for family and friends of victims.

....

It is not only rape survivors and their families, however, who experience and grieve the relationship changes that often take place in the aftermath of a loved one's trauma.

> *We had a great marriage and tons of friends, but since my wife's aneurysm, everything has changed. She's not the same, and I miss her; miss what we had. Once in a while I'll see a glimmer of who she was, and I'll let myself hope again. But things are getting worse. Her short-term memory is gone and she is very childlike and dependent now—which is hard, because she used to be the one who took care of me. I feel like I'm losing her bit by bit. I also feel like I'm losing me in the process.*

Grieving the Loss of Self

Perhaps the most complicated and confusing loss for family members is the intermittent loss of self that occurs when they put their own lives on hold in order to focus on their traumatized loved one's needs and problems. Many of us—especially women—were taught to take a backseat to others and try to please at all costs—even when the costs are high and eventually take their toll in bouts of depression and self-doubt and a pattern of codependency.

I use the word *codependency* knowing full well that it is a loaded term that some critics maintain is just another way to blame those who exhibit noble qualities of love and self-sacrifice. After all, being sensitive to another's feelings and caring for others are qualities we admire and try to embrace. But taken to extreme, these behaviors can become unhealthy.

Melody Beattie is credited for coming up with the term in her 1986 book *Codependent No More,* in which she describes codependents as people who become so obsessed with other people's feelings and behaviors that they—in an effort to control or fix another's behavior—lose sight of what they themselves are feeling or doing. Giving up this illusion of control is an integral step in achieving a healthy balance in relationships. It is true that being loving, giving, and nurturing are admirable qualities. We just need to balance that with taking time to love and nurture ourselves too. Often that means letting go of the idea that we have the power to change anyone.

This is what our grandparents were trying to get us to understand when they told us, "You can lead a horse to water, but you can't make it drink." We can guide and we can nag others, but we cannot script their lives or control how they will act or react. We can plot and plan our own lives, yet the unexpected happens. We can buckle our own and our children's seat belts, and drive as carefully as possible, but we have no control over the careless driver who veers into our lane and smashes into our car.

There's a joke in Twelve Step circles about how you know you're a codependent when you have a near-death experience and someone else's life flashes before your eyes. It is often easier to put another's needs ahead of our own, but the more we do that, the more difficult it becomes to define who we are and what our needs are independent of our loved one's. They usually don't ask for that level of attention, and we may not give it all the time. When we do, however, our loved one may often feel weighted down and a little smothered by our "selfless" devotion.

I got used to letting Michael's issues overshadow my life, but the more I focused on him and his trauma, the greater my resentment became. Several years before he was diagnosed with PTSD, Michael began writing a memoir, which he published just before my father died. I so vividly remember the day of Dad's death. I was at his side when he died in the early morning hours, but left my parents' house to drive, without any sleep, to be at Michael's side when he gave a reading from his book. I never thought to ask him to postpone it; I just set aside my grief and tried as best I could to get through the event. Now we both look upon that time with regret, but we understand so much more clearly how the pattern was set for Michael's needs to take precedence.

I also understand now how grief accumulates when you don't give each loss the attention it deserves, and how a stockpile of losses can lead to depression. Fortunately, some loving friends in whom I confided urged me to get help, and a great grief therapist gave me a safe place to cry, complain, worry, and rage, which allowed me to "empty my cup" and be more present and *genuinely* supportive of Michael when he took a medical leave to do his own intense therapy.

It is normal—and sometimes necessary—to put our lives on hold and focus on a traumatized loved one. Yet it is important to acknowledge how dramatically their trauma has changed our lives, making it our trauma too. We may choose to give up our time and a piece of ourselves to tend to their psychological or physical wounds, but there is still loss in the midst of that choice, and it is good to grieve that fact.

> *I was at work when a coworker told us there had been an explosion downtown and to turn on the TV. I immediately recognized the Murrah Building, and I knew where my husband's office was. All I saw was rubble. I think an event like the Oklahoma City bombing magnifies who we are and the traits we already possess. Sometimes it's great and sometimes it's not. I just knew that if the bomb didn't kill him the moment it went off he would be okay because he is such a strong person. He did live, but his injuries were extensive, requiring 18 months of physical therapy. He went back to work too early (after 43 days), but he felt so responsible for that building and the people in it. I felt my role at that point was to do whatever he needed. I never had control over him anyway. He's a very strong individual, but he was so physically and emotionally fragile. I had never seen him vulnerable.*
>
> *I know I should have gotten counseling, but my mother tapes clicked in, and I simply did what I thought I "should" do. I felt like I needed permission to get angry about things or say, "I just*

don't want to talk about it right now." I had no sense of self. About six months after the bombing, I had a doctor's appointment and my family physician who knew me very well asked how I was. "I have the strangest feeling," I told him. "I feel homesick." He said, "You're not crazy; your life is totally different from a few months ago; you're essentially mourning something you lost," and he put me on antidepressants. I didn't think I was entitled to have any mental stress is what it boils down to because I wasn't there.

When I saw the pictures from 9/11, my heart sank because I thought, "I know what the next years of their lives are going to be like." My heart immediately went to families who were losing people and to survivors and their families. I wanted to tell them not what to do, but to say, "It's happened before and we're on the other side of it now, so take heart. There is another side." We got the opportunity later to talk to them about how survivors and their families are victims too and how they do have a place in the story.

....

HONORING YOUR GRIEF

In his book *This Thing Called Grief: New Understandings of Loss*, Thomas Ellis emphasizes that "suffering alone does not teach. Time does *not* heal all wounds." Ellis offers tools and skills that can help people who have suffered a loss deal with their changing world. Following are a few ideas that are adapted from his book:

- Find companions for your journey through grief—those who get it (clergy, friends, family members, and so on), who truly care about you and who validate your personal grief process.
- Make time for grief by acknowledging it and spending time each day taking care of yourself.
- Tell yourself it is okay to feel a mix of emotions. Discover different ways to externalize your thoughts and feelings of

grief. "Talking, crying, and laughing are okay. Loss is the problem, not you," Ellis says.

- Gather information and become an expert about your loss—it may help reduce your anxiety.
- Name what is lost and what is not. "Clarifying your multiple losses and recognizing both what is left and what may come can lead to hope."
- Take a break from your grief. "Realize that you can't do this alone. Do what you can and not what others think or say you should do. Promote a sense of calm and healing."
- Embrace imperfection. "Realize that you don't have all the answers. You will continue to make good and bad choices. When it feels as if you can't make any more decisions, don't."
- Find places of sanctuary—peaceful and nourishing environments in and out of your home that allow you to fulfill your need for peace, quiet, and escape.

"Remember that you won't simply 'get over' your grief. Rather, it sits on your shoulder. But if you periodically turn your head and look at it straight on, the honest acknowledgment of your pain will bring relief. Grief is hard work, and it will take as long as it takes. . . . Grieving can become a sacred and creative time for you to discover who you are and how you choose to transform your life. Many have discovered that they can hold on to two opposing ideas—grief and hope—at the same time. You can too."

—Adapted from *This Thing Called Grief:
New Understandings of Loss* by Thomas M. Ellis

....

Green Grief

I've learned some of my most important grief lessons from dying loved ones. Before my forty-five-year-old cousin died from cancer, she told me how angry she and her husband were at each other. "I'm mad at him because he gets to live, and he's mad at me for dying," she said, teaching me how we are containers for all of it: the sadness, the joy, the anger, and the confusion.

We also talked about how difficult it was to put words to feelings. She wanted to talk to her four sons about her death and dying, but all of them were afraid to have "the conversation." "You'd think if I was able to talk to them about sex by putting a condom on a banana, I could talk to them about this!" she laughed. That's right, she laughed, and in doing so, gave all of us permission to laugh with her—another important lesson.

Thanks to another young dying friend, I now think of grief as green, like spring in Minnesota, with seeds of transition and hope buried within its dark soil. I visited her one dark and rainy August day, and found her content but in the confused state I had gotten used to since the discovery of her malignant and inoperable star-shaped brain tumor she dubbed "Stella." "Everything is GREEN. Today is a GREEN day," she pronounced, despite the dreariness outside. And then she directed, "Take this down. Rhonda Marie Carlson O'Gorman says, 'You must follow your fear.'"

She had recently taken to referring to herself in the third person, and I wondered if that was her way of reinforcing to herself and to others that, despite cancer, she was still Rhonda, with all the identities the various monikers conveyed (individual, daughter, and wife) intact. Now she assumed the role of teacher, and I, her obedient pupil, took out a little notebook from my purse. "Did you get that?" she persisted. "It is very important."

C. S. Lewis wrote, "No one ever told me that grief felt so like fear." I think that is the connection Rhonda was making. She and my cousin reinforced for me that we are unique and complex beings with complex feelings that change as we change. We are not one emotion like grief or one diagnosis like PTSD or cancer. It's all there, and if we peel back the veneer of our humanness we just might catch a glimpse of that green glimmer of hope.

While training to become a therapist, I worked with a group of Southeast Asian women refugees with PTSD who met weekly. They used their skills and cultural legacy to create individual traditional story cloths of their refugee experience and mourn their losses. Months of talking, sewing, and sharing came together when the individual cloths were joined to make a huge quilt-like wall hanging of their collective experience. I always smile when I remember the simple words of wisdom of one of these women. In her lovely, slow, and deliberate English, she said 'We cry. We laugh. We feel better.'

Grief is the emotion that flushes us out and makes room inside for healing. Allowing grief is a way to befriend ourselves—even when we don't understand it, when it doesn't make sense, or when we just feel sad with no way of explaining the feeling. The more we work through our feelings of loss and grief, the easier it becomes to reclaim or reframe what we have lost in the wake of a loved one's trauma. Be tender with yourselves as you do this sacred work in your time and in your own way. Cry. Laugh. Be angry. Follow your fear toward hope. And feel better.

....

A BLESSING A DAY

Make room to honor grief, but take time to notice the treasures each day holds in the midst of loss. Remember that old song that had the line, "Just count your blessings instead of sheep, and you'll go to sleep counting your blessings"? When I was in a slump, a friend suggested that I start a "Blessing a Day Journal" and every night write down the gifts I had been given that day. I got a special little book and wrote "My Blessings" on the cover. Each night I'd record things like "Beautiful sunset. The quality of light through the morning mist. The laughter of children in the park. The call from my mom saying she's proud of me."

After about a week, I was looking at the world differently. Instead of feeling irritated when it rained, I noticed how the rain glistened and danced on the window. Spiderwebs intrigued me. People delighted me. No matter how angry, sad, or frustrated I got during the day, my spirits would lift at day's end when I took the time to write down the gifts I had been given. And I'd often awaken greedy to see what the new day held.

Take a minute to review your day. Use your five senses (hearing, seeing, feeling, smelling, and tasting) to help you remember the good things you experienced. Did you hear people interacting in a special way? What did you notice in nature? Did your child hug you or show you affection? Did you eat a delicious meal with a friend? Did you laugh? Did you learn?

You may want to get a special little notebook for your blessings. You might want to start a "family blessings" journal in which each member can record a gift and see how all your blessings multiply when they are recorded together.

CHAPTER 3

What about Me?
The Importance of Self-Care

The Peace of Wild Things

When despair for the world grows in me
and I wake in the night at the least sound
in fear of what my life and my children's lives may be,
I go and lie down where the wood drake
rests in his beauty on the water, and the great heron feeds.
I come into the peace of wild things
who do not tax their lives with forethought
of grief. I come into the presence of still water.
And I feel above me the day-blind stars
waiting with their light. For a time
I rest in the grace of the world, and am free.

—WENDELL BERRY*

I HATE TO FLY, so I am one of those nervous airplane passengers who reads all the emergency instructions and listens intently to flight attendants when they demonstrate how to put on an

---

*Copyright © 1999 by Wendell Berry from *The Selected Poems of Wendell Berry*. Reprinted by permission of Counterpoint.

oxygen mask. "Put on your own mask before you help others," they remind us. In his poetic way, Wendell Berry urges us to do the same thing: stop, rest, and catch your breath when you are feeling overwhelmed, fearful, and worried. As the Bible says, restore your soul by still waters. This is the essence of self-care: be tender with yourself so you can be more compassionate toward others.

Self-care might seem like a lofty goal for those whose lives have been uprooted by trauma. When trauma strikes a loved one, or when the effects of trauma build to a crescendo over time, family and friends are thrust into the role of caregiver—a role they probably aren't prepared to assume. I remember telling a friend that I felt lost in the "bewilderness" when Michael was diagnosed with PTSD. In an effort to do everything they can for their loved one, caregivers frequently neglect their own needs. Things are already out of balance because of the trauma itself, and as more and more focus is directed toward their loved one, this imbalance grows even greater. In the words of one firefighter, "Sometimes your 'trauma trunk' just gets too full."

We're so worried about my cousin who has been trying his best to care for his partner who was diagnosed with PTSD from the effects of a chronic illness. On top of everything else, they had a house fire and lost everything and had to move out for ten months, so now they're dealing with that trauma too. He's got to handle all the insurance problems, the house reconstruction— everything—by himself. They live in a little town four hours away, so they're pretty isolated. He sounded so down and exhausted when we last spoke with him and scared us a little when he said, "I don't think I can do this any longer."

Whether a loved one's trauma symptoms manifest immediately or show up years later, education and good self-care are essential tools for coping with the shock wave effects of trauma. Dormant symptoms that could reemerge after an event or a sudden personal loss might be milder and more temporary if you and your loved one have prepared yourselves by learning about triggers and ways to minimize the damage of retraumatization.

While our individual circumstances are as varied as our individual stories, I am willing to bet that if you made a list of things to take care of today, *you* would not be on it. Caring for a trauma survivor with deep psychological wounds is a demanding and often thankless task because at times they may be incapable of feeling anything, let alone gratitude. They might be sullen or angry, and that anger may be directed at you because they haven't yet uncovered the root of it or recognized it as a trauma symptom. They may not be able or willing to work through difficult problems or interactions in a loving way with you and other family members. They may also be in denial about their post-traumatic symptoms.

> *My husband has PTSD, and sometimes I feel like a single parent. One day when I had a lot of errands, I asked him if he would vacuum. I came home after dropping my daughter off and he still hadn't done it. When I asked him about it, he blew up, yelling, "I've always gotta do everything on your time." He grabbed the vacuum and just kept shouting, "Happy now? Happy now?" If I didn't have God, I'd be locked up right now. I suffer from depression and anxiety issues, yet I'm working full time, running the household, doing yard work, and trying to raise children.*

Balance and Boundaries

After many years of relative silence about his combat experience, there came a time when it seemed like all Michael thought or talked about was Vietnam. On the surface, I appeared to be the picture of encouragement, but things got out of balance. My resentment grew in direct proportion to my "selflessness." I gave up my computer and office so he could write about war. I stayed out of his way. Sometimes he'd wake me up late at night to read me what he'd written, and I'd listen, both as a supportive spouse and as a writing teacher. When

I tried to talk about my feelings or my writing, he'd often cut me off, interrupt me, or tell me to go to sleep. I shrank further into his shadow, wondering, when will it be *my* turn?

Trauma throws lives and family dynamics off balance and can shift the healthiest of boundaries. *Appropriate* boundaries are the way we differentiate ourselves from others. They protect and preserve our individuality and help us keep our self-esteem intact. When trauma comes, appropriate boundaries are easier to describe than they are to set. Trauma survivors might establish rigid boundaries, shutting out those who care for them the most. On the other hand, their family and friends might have few boundaries or forget about boundaries altogether as they focus more and more on their loved one and less and less on themselves.

Messages we received as children about rules and boundaries might be reactivated, and we find ourselves responding to the trauma in much the same way we saw our parents and even grandparents handle crises when we were kids. I came from an enmeshed family system with weak boundaries where members got all tangled up and involved in each other's problems and lives. Michael, however, came from a disengaged family system where isolation and secrets were the norm. As his trauma symptoms grew more severe, he retreated. In an attempt to rescue him, I invaded. Michael was too numb to know his needs, let alone express them. I knew my needs, but suppressed them in favor of what I imagined his needs to be.

Healthy boundary setting often starts by reminding yourself that *you* didn't cause your loved one's trauma, and—as much as you may want to—*you* cannot cure it. Remember the Serenity Prayer? Change what you can change.

My brother has definitely challenged my boundaries and tested my boundary-setting skills. I think this is because of his PTSD. But the more I learn about trauma, the better I'm getting at setting appropriate boundaries with him. It's still hard, but I keep trying because it's important for me to have a relationship with my brother.

Simply put, when we set boundaries, we set limits. We learn when to say no, and when we say yes, we do so out of choice, not guilt or obligation. As we become more aware of our own needs and feelings, we become more respectful of others' needs, feelings, and limitations. We concentrate more on improving ourselves and less on controlling or fixing a loved one. Setting boundaries is such a grown-up thing to do!

A dear friend modeled healthy boundary setting on a recent visit. When the National Guard fired shots on May 4, 1970, that killed four Kent State University students in Ohio, he was close enough to see one of them fall, and rushed to her side to help. She died as he tried to hold her neck together until the ambulance came, and he still harbors the memories of that traumatic experience. When we asked him to join us at a rally a while ago, he grew quiet and seemed a little anxious, but was able to explain how political gatherings are one of the triggers that reignite the trauma of that day decades ago. He didn't make up an excuse or risk a relapse of symptoms by thinking he had to come along to please us. We so appreciated his honesty, and because he was so clear, we were able to give him our *genuine* support. He honored his boundaries by staying home; we honored ours by going.

We take care of ourselves when we accept responsibility for the consequences of our own actions and reactions, and sort out what we can and cannot control. By taking personal responsibility, we move beyond blame and shame. We are bound to make mistakes, but we don't punish ourselves unmercifully for them; we learn from our mistakes and move on. We learn to quiet that incessant chatterbox inside our head that drones on and on with negative self-talk, and replace it instead with a loving voice that convinces us we are strong and worthy. We understand that we have choices, and that we can choose to take the path that contributes most to our personal growth and happiness.

LOVING YOURSELF

We can give love to our traumatized loved one, our friends, our family, and *ourselves* all at the same time. We befriend and care for ourselves best when we recognize we have the basic right to

- Be ourselves
- Be treated with respect, as capable, competent, and imperfect adults
- Set limits and establish appropriate boundaries
- Refuse requests without feeling guilty or selfish
- Feel and express our own emotions
- Ask for affection and help
- Change our minds, make mistakes, and admit when we don't know, don't agree, or don't understand
- Decide when we are responsible, what we are responsible for, and how we choose to accept responsibility
- Protect ourselves
- Grow and learn

If you have difficulty remembering or believing your personal rights, copy this list, add any more you can think of, and carry it in your purse or billfold to remind you that you are a worthwhile and deserving person.

Signs and Symptom of Stress

I have a cartoon on my office wall of a zebra gazing back at his rear end with alarm because his stripes are coming off, unraveling like a ribbon. The caption, "I think I'm having stress!" makes me smile and serves as a reminder that unless I take care of myself, stress can creep in, threaten my health, and possibly lead to depression.

We know from the volumes that have been written on stress management that we all need to get enough sleep, eat nutritiously, and exercise. Yet naps, vegetables, and yoga are probably the last things on your mind as you try to keep your household running smoothly in the aftermath of a loved one's trauma. You may have growing financial concerns if your loved one is unable to work. Your own job performance may suffer because your home environment is chaotic. Your loved one's insomnia or nightmares might be disrupting your sleep, and you find yourself exhausted during the day. You might be angry or frustrated because your loved one refuses to get treatment for post-traumatic symptoms. Or—if they are getting treatment— trauma issues could seem to loom even larger as they devote necessary time and energy to therapy and you are left to deal with day-to-day family matters.

> *We worried constantly about my sister when her young son was diagnosed with terminal cancer. My brother-in-law went to pieces and couldn't work, so in addition to the emotional turmoil she was having, she had to worry about how she was going to pay the bills, keep her job, care for her son and her other two kids, and keep her marriage together. The family tried to help her, but we all live across the country, so it all fell on her.*

Left untended, long-term stress can lead to serious health problems. Among other things, stress can raise blood pressure, suppress the immune system, increase the risk of heart attack and stroke, give you headaches and stomach problems, disrupt your sleep, or lead to eating disorders and depression.

Review the following list of common warning signs and symptoms of stress to see how close you are to stress overload:

Cognitive Symptoms
- Memory problems
- Inability to concentrate
- Lapses in judgment
- Pessimism

- Anxiousness
- Constant worry

Physical Symptoms
- Aches and pains
- Diarrhea or constipation
- Nausea, dizziness
- Chest pain, rapid heartbeat
- Frequent colds

Emotional Symptoms
- Moodiness
- Irritability or short temper
- Agitation, inability to relax
- Feelings of being overwhelmed
- Sense of loneliness and isolation
- General unhappiness

Behavioral Symptoms
- Eating too much or too little
- Sleeping too much or too little
- Isolating yourself from others
- Using alcohol, cigarettes, or other drugs to relax
- Acting out nervous habits, such as nail biting

It's important to see a doctor for a full medical evaluation if you are experiencing a number of these symptoms. The longer you ignore them, the more serious they can become.

Think of stress as the tension on a violin string. If there is too much tension, the string snaps. If the string is too loose, the sound is listless and hollow. Again, it comes back to balance. A little stress can energize us and keep us sharp; too much stress can break us. When we tune into our bodies and our minds, slow down a little, and take care of ourselves, we strike a balance. We realize that we can compose the music of our own lives.

Stress Management

We can't eliminate stress completely, but we can learn to identify it and reduce it using some simple tools of self-care. Just as parents give their children a timeout when they get overstimulated, we can give ourselves a timeout when a stressful situation arises by counting to ten, breathing evenly and deeply, or perhaps changing the subject—all strategies that can release and shift the tension of the moment. Adding something beautiful to our lives like music or flowers, and taking time to breathe in and focus on the beauty, can also create an emotional shift.

> *Gardening is very powerful for me—digging and connecting physically with the earth to participate in the creation of something beautiful or nourishing is very healing. It is like trauma had the power to take away the ground beneath me. Feeling and actively living with that ground brings some core strength within me "back home."*

If possible, try to get outside at least once a day for a short walk or a quiet moment. Wear comfortable and loose clothing whenever possible. Try to eat nutritious and regular meals, and avoid abusing alcohol or drinking too much caffeine. Try to get enough sleep. Find a safe place to feel, express, and embrace your feelings. Consider a warm bath or getting a pedicure. Watch a light-hearted movie, and laugh. Laugh often.

Another stress-busting technique is contained in the two-letter word "no." It's perfectly okay to decline an invitation occasionally, to tell the PTA president you aren't able to chair this year's fun fair but you would be happy to bake some bars or help in some other way.

> *When my husband was recovering, the old tapes of "you have to be nice to people and be a good hostess" got replayed and I never considered I had the right or choice to say I wanted to be alone. There was a solid stream of people at the hospital, but they pressed against the wall, afraid to come close. I guess they just needed to see him alive.*

It's all right to ask friends and relatives not to call during dinner, and it's all right to tell someone you will call them back if it's not a convenient time. It's fine to ask people not to stop by without notice. It's even permissible to say no to your children when they beg for an unnecessary toy or pair of designer jeans. And when you're dog-tired and overwhelmed, it's okay to say no to household chores once in a while, and yes to a long soak in the tub or a few more hours of sleep.

Stress's Cousin: Depression

Too much stress for too long a time can make us more vulnerable to depression—a common yet serious medical illness that can affect all aspects of life if left untreated. Symptoms of depression, which mirror the symptoms of stress, last for more than a few weeks and can make it difficult to function in daily life. Depressed individuals might feel hopeless, disinterested in things that used to be pleasurable, or even suicidal. When we are depressed, it is also common to be plagued with cognitive distortions—what those in Twelve Step recovery groups often call "stinking thinking."

The idea that our feelings result from the messages we give ourselves is at the heart of cognitive therapy. In *Feeling Good: The New Mood Therapy*, Dr. David D. Burns explains how our thoughts or perceptions (our "cognitions") can direct our feelings. Until I got help with my depression, I didn't realize how distorted my thinking was. *I* made sense to *me*.

When we slip into distorted thinking, we have a tendency to see the world as black and white—we live in an *always* or *never* world. Burns writes that distorted thinkers are often convinced others are looking down on them, and jump to negative conclusions. (If a friend doesn't call or if someone isn't paying close enough attention to you, they *must* hate you.) Distorted thinkers think at the extremes. They might magnify their faults out of proportion while they play down any strengths they have. They may also confuse their emotions for facts. It's an "I feel therefore it is" approach to life. (If I'm angry, you *must* have done something contrary.) Burns maintains people in despair also tend to beat themselves up for what they think they should and shouldn't do, ultimately creating self-loathing, shame, and guilt because they feel they are constantly falling short of their expectations. Distorted thinkers also label themselves based on their failures (I should have done a better job) and take responsibility for any negative (If my traumatized loved one withdraws, I must have done something wrong).

Distorted thinkers don't only blame themselves. To feel better about themselves, they often blame others for their unhappiness. (The clerk at the store put me in a bad mood, my friend made me miss exercise class, my boss made me look stupid, the mechanic hates women, God is punishing me.) They avoid taking responsibility by holding others responsible. But they gradually feel worse as their list of scapegoats gets longer, their trust level plummets, and their sadness intensifies.

When my therapist suggested I read Burns' book, I felt like a curtain had been lifted. There wasn't a wizard behind it, only a mirror, only me pulling the levers, controlling the thoughts. I was both elated and terrified to realize how powerful my thoughts were, and how negative or distorted thoughts could paralyze me. It was so much easier to blame Michael or PTSD for all my problems than to accept responsibility for my own thoughts, feelings, actions, and reactions.

The good news is that depression is a very treatable condition. The Web site www.depression-screening.org offers a confidential screening for depression that can help you determine if you should seek professional help. As with any other illness, you should see your doctor if you think you might be depressed. Mental Health America (www.nmha.org) also provides free information on depression, its treatment, and local screening sites.

....

HOW WELL ARE YOU TAKING CARE OF YOURSELF?

It's a good idea to pause every now and again to take your emotional, physical, mental, and spiritual pulse in order to track how well you are taking care of yourself. Take a minute to reflect upon the previous week and ask yourself:

- **Am I honoring my body?**
Have I listened to its aches, tensions, and feelings? Did I take time to rest when I was tired? Did I get some exercise? Did I eat balanced and healthy meals?
- **Am I honoring my mind?**
Have I taken the time to read a good book, take an interesting class, or learn something new? Was I able to exchange ideas and talk about opinions with a friend?
- **Am I honoring my emotions?**
Was I able to express my feelings in my journal or to another person? Have I spent quality time with someone this week? Did I take time to play and laugh? Did I give myself time to cry when I needed to?
- **Am I honoring my spirit and soul?**
Have I spent time in prayer, meditation, or solitary thought? Have I taken the time to be quiet with myself and with nature? Have I read something inspirational or listened to beautiful music?

Keep this list handy and refer to it often. Use it as a reminder to keep your life in balance.

....

Nurturing Yourself

It may be taking every ounce of energy and patience you possess to juggle day-to-day responsibilities as you support your traumatized loved one, and the idea of carving out time for yourself might even sound like one more thing to add to your "to do" list. Even if your loved one is getting psychological or physical help from outside sources, you are no doubt being called upon to be the head, heart, and hands for your family while your loved one is recovering from the effects of trauma. On the days you feel your life is falling apart, think of self-care as the glue that helps hold it all together. (But try to practice it on the in-between days too).

Pause for a moment and think about how much time you devote to your loved one's care and trauma-related problems. Now think about how much time you spend caring for yourself. Are things too far out of balance?

Pay It Forward was a popular movie in 2000 in which a young boy urges people to do three good deeds for others when a good deed is done for them. His rationale was that if everyone did this, kindness would spread and the world would become a better place. How about "paying it inward" by doing three nice things for yourself today? The care, concern, and love you show your loved one are valuable and tender gifts. Now it's time to be tender with yourself and allow that self-care to grow exponentially. When we are kind to ourselves, our capacity for kindness to others magnifies.

Ask for, and Accept, Help

Did you hear the one about the guy in the flood? As the rains came day after the day, the river on which his house was located rose higher and higher until the authorities finally gave the word to evacuate. Neighbor after neighbor packed their belongings and left their homes, but the man refused to go with them. "God will take care of me," he told them confidently when they begged him to leave. "I'll just stay here and pray. I'm sure God will save me." The water rose higher, rushing into the first floor of the house. Undaunted, the man went to his second-story bedroom to pray some more. When people in a boat came by pleading with him to leave, the stubborn man shouted from his second-story window, "Thank you, but I'm going to stay. God will take care of me." And still the river kept rising, finally forcing the man to seek refuge on his rooftop. As he sat on his roof praying, a helicopter flew overhead, dangling a rope ladder for the man to climb. But the stubborn man waved the helicopter away, shouting, "I'll be okay. God will take care of me." Still, the river was more stubborn than the man and it rose high enough to swallow both the house and the man, who still sat praying upon the roof. He was a little miffed when he got to heaven. "God, I prayed and prayed. Why didn't you save me?" God, looking just a tad impatient, answered, "I sent the sheriff, a boat, and a helicopter. What more did you expect?"

Sometimes we're like the stubborn man. We get so distracted waiting for help to arrive that we don't notice when it's right before our eyes. Our pride, fear, uncertainty, or just plain exhaustion can overwhelm us and keep us isolated on our rooftops. But if we reach out and embrace the hands that are extended to us, wonderful things can happen. Community can happen.

> *I was retired as a NYC firefighter because of a lung condition when 9/11 happened, and had just finished training in massage, body, and emotional release work. This saved me, because it gave me the chance to use this at the Family Assistance Center at Pier 94. Everyone forgets that each one of the survivors is just the first domino that sets hundreds of family dominoes on their own journeys of pain. Take each life lost on 9/11 and multiply that by ten or twenty family members, then multiply that by all their friends, and you have a world of pain and trauma to heal.*

Charles Dickson, a North Carolina clergyman and chemistry instructor, urges us to take some lessons from the geese when it comes to getting help. He writes that whenever a goose falls out of the flock's V formation, it suddenly feels the increased air resistance of trying to fly alone, so it quickly learns to get back into formation to take advantage of the drafting power of the bird in front of it. By flying together this way, the whole flock can fly much farther. "If we have as much sense as the geese, we will be willing to accept help when we need it as well as lend help to others when they need it," writes Dickson.

There are three basic steps in asking for help. The first step is to identify your problem or need or fear. Often just naming a pain or difficulty is a release because by doing so, you give yourself permission to be vulnerable, to be less than perfect. When we expect perfection, we operate in a world of illusion. We judge ourselves by impossible standards and berate ourselves when we fail to meet our unreachable goals.

After you have a pretty good idea of why you need help, the second step is to figure out who can most appropriately give you the help you need—understanding that you cannot predict the responses you'll receive. Some people may disappoint you by not being readily available, and others will totally surprise you by their willingness to come to your aid.

Think about aspects of your life and your family's lives, and brainstorm a list of people or organizations you could contact if a need arose in a particular area. Enlist your loved one in compiling this list, so you'll have it if an emergency arises and they are unable to help. Who would help you with a house or car repair? Who can take care of the children if you need child care?

It is also fine—and a good idea—to ask your loved one during a calm period who you should call if a trauma-related, emotional crisis arises. Think of this person as having attributes similar to those of a sponsor for a recovering person. It should be someone who is familiar with your loved one's trauma—perhaps another trauma survivor who is solid in their own recovery (although the trauma experience may differ from your loved one's)—who would know ahead of time who to call and where to go for help.

> *My girlfriend is not a vet, but she has PTSD, and one night she had a pretty scary meltdown. I called my vet friend with PTSD for help, and he knew just what to do. He came over immediately with a list of emergency numbers in his hand. He was able to calm her down and we didn't need them, but it was great knowing we both had that kind of help when we needed it.*

The third step is to actually ask for the help you need. To ask for help is to practice humility, a noble virtue. Philosopher Simone Weil called humility "compassion directed to oneself." You are worthy of tenderness, and you are entitled to compassion from others and from yourself.

Be as specific and as clear as you can be in your request for help. And if people aren't able to help you, accept their answer at face value. They might have other commitments, or they might not be able to help for some complicated and personal reasons unknown to you. Think about the times a favor has been asked of you and the times you have not been able to do that favor for whatever reason. If person A can't help you, say "thank you" anyway and call person B. If person B can't help, think about an organization or professional you could turn to.

> When our thirty-year-old son was diagnosed with a stage four melanoma, I felt helpless. People asked what they could do, but I was too overwhelmed to think of anything to tell them. Then I got a note from a friend with a list of choices like, deliver a meal, take a walk with me, bring over a movie, get some dishes I can throw, meet me in New York for his surgery. I loved her for offering such tangible things instead of the vague "if there is anything I can do," which puts more of a burden on the care-giver. Embedded in that generous list was a sense of humor and warmth that made it possible for me to accept her offer to be with me while he had his surgery.

Enlist family members to help you with household chores and meals—including the trauma survivor if she or he is able. If you have kids, teach them how to make their own breakfast, how to set the table, load and empty the dishwasher, and clean their rooms. Praise them for their competence. Even small children can be assigned household responsibilities that can increase as they grow older.

Keeping up routines can reassure *all* family members that there is normalcy even in the midst of abnormal situations. Honor your traditions such as Friday night pizza and home movies. If Saturday is chore day, try to keep to that schedule. Attend religious services if that is what your family has always done. Such familiar patterns give your loved one a solid foundation on which to build some healing strategies. If something happens to change your plans, try to be flexible and carry on with the routine the next week.

When my wife was first diagnosed with PTSD, we all tiptoed around her, trying to give her space, keep things quiet, and do everything for her. Finally, one day she told us that our attempts to be the perfect family were driving her nuts and making her feel even weirder than she already did. We all laughed, and got back to being our regular, imperfect selves.

Stay Connected—with Others and with Yourself

Try to make space and time every day (or several days each week) to catch up on what each family member is doing or feeling. These needn't be forced encounter groups. Just carving out time to be together without distractions often opens the door to casual check-ins and gives you an opportunity to gauge how everyone is handling the aftereffects of your loved one's trauma. Turning off the phone or not answering the phone during dinner is a start. Or try playing a board game or cards during the week and see what conversations are sparked.

When our daughter was very seriously injured in a violent attack, it turned our family upside down. One of our biggest challenges as parents has been to continue to balance the attention we give her with attention to our two younger children. We were in a local malt shop one afternoon when a young mother and her two children in the next booth caught my attention. After they got settled and placed their order, the mom turned to her son and daughter and asked, "What did you learn today, and what made you laugh?" The question seemed comfortable and routine, a daily practice for this family. With this simple ritual, this mother was giving her children permission to express themselves and giving them the message that they—and their thoughts and feelings— were important. We adopted the same daily practice, and it's worked wonders with all of the kids.

Of course, there will be days when your best intentions will have to be thrown out the window. Try to be gentle with yourself and your family during such detours and accept them as just that—temporary bends in the road, not an exploded highway you can never return to again.

Finally, remember to *schedule*—not wish or try or hope, but actually set aside—time for just yourself. If you have kids and your loved one is unable or unwilling to babysit, barter child care with a friend and give yourself a night off. You might want to use Julia Cameron's idea of making an "artist's date" with yourself. In her book *The Artist's Way: A Spiritual Path to Higher Creativity,* Cameron instructs us to set aside a block of time every week reserved only for ourselves. You might take a walk or go out to dinner with a friend, visit a museum, or curl up with a good book.

As a wife of a PTSD spouse, I definitely get my down times, more than I would like to admit as my hubby refuses to get help. We also have a young son, and I have to referee . . . [from the time] my husband comes home from work until the time our son goes to bed. They consistently try to battle each other then come to me. I have learned that shower time is MY time. I have to watch my stress and anxiety, as I get frequent migraine headaches and then all three of us are grouchy! And I get as much sleep as I can, after "my" time on the computer.

Treat your time as sacred. Write it on your family's engagement calendar in bold letters, and then highlight it with a neon magic marker. You might just convince yourself you deserve it, and you are modeling something invaluable to your children: the importance of tenderness to self.

Organize

Take time to make time. Prioritize. Consciously choose what you need and want to do each day so you are spending more of your time the way you want to spend it. Sometimes it may be worth it to stay up late to clean or to fix that leaky pipe if these things are getting to you. At other times, you may temporarily opt for messiness and a bucket in order to do something enjoyable or get some sleep.

Make written lists of your daily activities, and label the most urgent things you have to do. Cross off things as you accomplish them. Try to schedule appointments and errands back-to-back so you can consolidate trips. Put a family engagement calendar on the wall or refrigerator to record each member's activities and appointments.

Plan ahead. Try to set aside one day a week for shopping and other errands and chart your course ahead of time for maximum efficiency. Use the Internet to find a store that has a particular item in stock, rather than traveling all over town to locate it. If you're in charge of finances, try to pay your bills at one time, and file receipts immediately.

....

SET YOUR OWN PRIORITIES

Listing your priorities is a way to make sure that your agenda is truly your agenda—not your loved one's agenda or your children's agenda or your boss' agenda or your friends' agenda.

Take a minute and write out the answers to the following questions:

- What do I need to accomplish today?
- What do I need or want to do for myself today?
- What do I want to do for or with others today?
- How will I go about accomplishing what I need and want to get done?
- How will I allow room for flexibility?

This sort of tracking makes us aware of the fragility or strength of our commitments. We can see how we set out to do something and how we let ourselves get pulled aside.

As we observe the ebb and flow of our thoughts and actions, we realize how others are living with similar shifts and changes. Compassion grows. We learn to assess our decisions, to redirect and forgive ourselves and others for not being perfect.

....

Compassion Fatigue

My three-year-old grandsons gave me a refresher course in compassion not long ago on a sleepover when they were chatting over the sides of their porta-cribs like two friends over a backyard fence. One held a little fabric bunny, the other a shiny little purple lizard, and they were having a "conversation" with their respective toys. "Oh, look," said the lizard. "I only have one eye." "It is okay," assured the bunny. "I have a heart, but I have no eyes." "I feel better now," said the lizard.

Compassion literally means "to suffer with," and that is just what can happen to those who practice great empathy—they absorb the pain and trauma of others until they themselves become mentally, physically, and spiritually exhausted. This condition is often called "compassion fatigue." J. Colleen Breen, the author of *Making Changes: A Guidebook for Managing Life's Challenges*, describes it as a kind of "soul sadness" because there is an inner, core reality that closes down when people become so overwhelmed by the needs and concerns of others that they forget to take care of themselves.

Medical and mental health care professionals, emergency care workers, clergy, counselors, and volunteers who work with very sick or troubled people are particularly susceptible to compassion fatigue— as are family and friends of trauma survivors. Breen, a licensed social worker, says she has worked with thousands of caregivers who have so overextended themselves in the service of others that they suffer from "care-giving shutdown." They often become withdrawn and joyless, irritable, depressed, uninterested in intimacy and sex, and feel like they're "just going through the motions" of their lives or jobs with no sense of purpose or meaning. They might also employ what Breen calls negative coping skills, by turning to smoking, drinking, using drugs, or practicing addictive behaviors.

When additional stress from caring for a traumatized loved one is added to the mix of grief, worry, and empathy we've already got stored up inside ourselves from the cares and concerns of our day-to-day life and jobs, we become like overinflated balloons, ready to burst from all we are trying to contain. We might have nightmares, develop stress-related illnesses, or exhibit the other symptoms of compassion fatigue (which also are a lot like post-trauma symptoms).

> *We've been so worried about our friend who has been the primary caretaker for his wife. He refuses help and has been trying to handle everything himself. Finally, it got to be too much and he ended up in a hospital for a couple of days. He was so emotionally and physically exhausted that the doctors said his brain just shut down. He doesn't even remember going to the emergency room. Maybe this will be the turning point for both of them getting the help they need.*

Because compassion fatigue adversely affects body, mind, and spirit, it makes sense to concentrate on those areas when attempting to treat or prevent this condition. Overstressed caregivers need some kind of physical regimen to deal with the stress that settles in their bodies. It is equally important to take quiet time for reflection, prayer, or solitude and engage creatively with things other than caregiving. Ease your mind by turning off television or radio news and taking a break from newspapers when the weight of the world seems too much to bear. And take care of yourself by asking for help.

> *The families of persons with PTSD are increasingly vulnerable to divorce, domestic violence, aggression, depression, and anxiety.*

Support for family members is needed to prevent what is now re-
ferred to as compassion burden. Partners are vulnerable to over-
compensating for the trauma survivor and taking on unrealistic
levels of family responsibility. Family and friends become famil-
iar with the survivor's triggers and can exert inordinate energy
to manage or avoid them. In the face of trauma symptoms, they
may lose track of their own reality and their need for calm, rest,
fun, and care. A wise therapist once told me she no longer believes
there is such a thing as individual suffering. Families need to
create time and space away from the trauma.

Don't wait until the pipe breaks, the dog runs away, your child gets sick, or a relationship is in shambles to get a support network in place. Approach this task like a detective, uncovering clues and leads over time. Ask people at your children's school, your workplace, your grocery store, or your place of worship for ideas and informa- tion. Having these resources on hand will also help your loved one when they are feeling overwhelmed and can't think where to turn for help.

....

LISTING YOUR RESOURCES

Lists are a way to break down an often overwhelming whole into manageable parts. A list can be a summary of what you need, want, or have. It can also give you ideas for what you can do to get your needs met. A list is easy to add to and easy to alter as your situation and needs change. A list can also help you articulate your request when you need to ask for help.

Take a minute and list the people you would contact:

- To discuss a personal problem or fear
- When you need a tender hug or a soft shoulder for a good cry
- For child care

- For health care advice for you and your children
- For health care emergencies
- For financial or legal help
- For automobile advice or repair
- For household maintenance or advice
- For last-minute scheduling changes or conflicts (for example, who could pick your children up from school if you were at work and one of them got ill?)
- For scholastic advice or counseling for you or your children
- For spiritual advice or guidance
- For social interaction for you and your children
- To exercise or play with
- For laughter or consolation when you're "in the dumps"

Categorize your list in whatever way feels logical to you. Include addresses, phone numbers, and emails, and add back-up contacts whenever you think of them. Let people know you're compiling this network and ask them if it's all right to contact them when a need arises. Negotiate with friends to see if there is anything you can do in exchange for their help. Be creative. Barter services. Help the teenager next door with his math if he'll mow your lawn. Weed your mother's garden when she watches your children. This is mutuality. This is community in action.

CHAPTER 4

Self-Care II: Toward Healthy Interdependence and Dialogue

After a while you learn the subtle difference between holding a hand and chaining a soul.
After a while you learn that kisses aren't contracts, and pres-
ents aren't promises.
And you begin to accept your defeats with your head up and
your eyes ahead,
with the grace of an adult, and learn to build all of your roads
on today because tomorrow's ground is too uncertain for
plans, and futures have a way of falling down in midflight.
After a while you learn that even sunshine burns if you ask
too much.
So you plant your own garden and decorate your own soul,
instead of waiting for someone to bring you flowers.
And you learn that you really can endure, that you really are
strong, and you really do have worth.
And you learn, and you learn, and you learn . . .

—AUTHOR UNKNOWN (EXCERPTED)

MY MOTHER GAVE ME A COPY OF THIS ANONYMOUS POEM she
clipped from an old Ann Landers column years ago. I've always
liked its lovely honesty, but it also strikes me as a little sad and

isolating. Yes, it is good to "decorate your own soul" by practicing the basics of self-care. But, as was discussed in the last chapter, an important element of good self-care is asking for help and support from others. It is good—and necessary—to have quiet alone time in which to recharge your batteries for the demanding challenges that accompany a loved one's trauma. But we need to connect with others too. We need to be able to express our feelings and experience the healthy give-and-take of living in the world with others. Planting a garden (to use the poem's metaphor) can be a worthwhile meditative and solitary act, but it is also joyful to harvest our crops together and share in the bounty our efforts produced.

Twelve Step participants are often told, "When you're home by yourself, you're behind enemy lines," or "If you share your pain you cut it in half; if you don't you double it." Others may say, "My head is like a bad neighborhood and I shouldn't go in there alone," or "It isn't the load that weighs us down, it's the way we carry it." They realize the importance of having a healthy and honest support system—especially during times of stress and emotional turmoil. Millions of recovering people worldwide have also learned the benefits of telling their story and listening without judgment to the stories of others.

I view friendship as a verb, a fluid process that changes with time and experience. To me, the best relationships are those that consist of a mutual bond of respect, trust, and vulnerability that encourages healthy growth and acceptance. When it comes to trauma and its shock wave effects, some people will be receptive to listening to and learning from your experiences. Others will turn a deaf ear or discount the serious impact your loved one's trauma is having on you. Still others might be happy to help with home maintenance or meals, but they might not be able to give you emotional support for a host of possible reasons—one being that your story brings up painful memories of their own.

We need to take care of ourselves so we can compassionately care for others without getting emotionally and physically depleted.

Learning how to share deep feelings with others helps us listen more empathetically to our own inner voice and to others'—including our loved ones'.

> *My best friend knows me better than anyone and has always listened to me with an open heart and mind. I can talk about how my husband's trauma affects me without feeling whiney or guilty. Because she came from a family where secrecy was the rule, it's harder for her to talk about feelings. It took her years to tell me some of the things she went through as a kid, but eventually she did confide in me. Trusting me with her story was the biggest gift she ever gave me. Things feel so much more balanced now.*

When we share our feelings, we practice being vulnerable, one of the conditions of friendship. It is not easy to be vulnerable in a society where the myth of rugged individualism still looms large. As psychotherapist Terrence Real points out in his book *I Don't Want to Talk About It: Overcoming the Secret Legacy of Male Depression,* men are taught to deny vulnerability, reject expressivity, and deny the existence of trauma at a young age. On the other hand, women in our society are taught to pull pain inward and blame themselves when they feel bad, while men are conditioned to externalize their pain— blaming others or outside forces for their distress. When we risk being vulnerable, we give our friend or loved ones permission to be vulnerable too—which allows us to look more objectively at trauma and its effects. This is mutuality in action.

The Importance of Telling Your Story

There is a time to listen and a time to talk, and we achieve balance in relationships when we are able to do both. My dad, like many World War II combat veterans, didn't talk much about the war when I was young. In his last years, however, he began telling bits of stories that hinted at the trauma he carried for more than fifty years. By then, though, he delivered his anecdotes out of context and at odd times, and I was not a good listener. In between television shows, he'd sometimes dreamily mention the "German lad" he shot or talk briefly about the "poor souls" he witnessed being liberated at the Dachau concentration camp. At that point, Mom usually interrupted with her familiar, "Oh, Bob, the kids don't want to hear those stories."

I now realize that Mom probably didn't like Dad to talk about the war because she also carried invisible scars from those painful years. She was a young and very pregnant bride, home alone with a toddler, dealing with things like the unexpected death of her forty-two-year-old father-in-law, ration coupons, and all the other stresses of wartime—chief among them her constant dread that her husband would be killed or wounded in battle. She needed to tell her war stories too.

In her book *Storycatcher: Making Sense of Our Lives through the Power and Practice of Story*, Christina Baldwin talks about a country plagued by tribal wars where the guerilla armies of the hill people stole the boys of the valley people and forced them to fight against their own tribe. As she describes it:

> UNICEF heard of this atrocity and decided to buy back the children and reintroduce them to their villages. The UNICEF workers would drive into these remote villages with several boys who had been gone for two, three, four years; boys whose childhoods had been stolen, whose souls were wracked with the guilt of what they had done. They went to the tribal elders and asked them "We have brought them home to you, but they are not the same. What will you do?"
>
> "We will light a fire in the center of the village every night for a year," the elders replied. "The boys will be required to come and tell their stories and listen to the reactions of the villagers. We will weep together for what this war has done. We will talk until the war is talked out of them, until the sorrow is healed, until the fire is burned up."

I held this passage before me as I gathered stories for this book. When they are ready and when it is safe to do so, it can be helpful—and usually necessary—for trauma survivors and those who love them to tell their stories over and over until the trauma is "talked out of them." Each time they tell about their respective experiences and recount the damage trauma has caused, the event can lose a little more of its ability to disrupt lives. As a therapist who works with Iraq veterans told me, "Telling your story can be extremely healing and empowering for those who have experienced trauma, but you have to be careful so they aren't retraumatized. It's healthy to be able to feel things, and talking about pain is a huge step toward healing."

Sexual abuse survivors may have an especially difficult time talking about their trauma—especially if the abuse was incestuous. As Kristin Kunzman explains in her book *The Healing Way: Adult Recovery from Childhood Sexual Abuse,*

> It's natural to feel anxiety at telling others of your childhood abuse. You've spent years believing you had to protect that secret. If the abuse was incestuous, you may, by breaking the secret, feel disloyal to your family and feel exposed. But you have a right to share your secret with others and thereby lessen your pain. Keeping secrets and denying the abuse put you in danger of more abuse. Speaking out breaks the cycle. Keeping a secret, even for days or weeks, takes a lot of energy and conscious effort. Keeping a secret for years, first as a child, then as an adult, consumes amazing amounts of energy.

Here again, it is crucial that trauma survivors take good care of themselves by being intentional about telling their story. Kunzman advises that abuse survivors wait until they are further in recovery before they talk about their experience with their family, lest they be met with denial, disbelief, or a total lack of support: "When you break your silence for the first time, you need to tell someone who feels safe to you. The safest person is someone who won't judge you and who will listen to your story, however you decide to tell it. An old and trusted friend, a therapist, or a counselor might all be good choices."

In writing this book, I listened to trauma stories that took place as much as sixty years ago and as recently as last year, and I learned how those traumas continue to affect families and friends. While the stories had found a place in people's lives (as opposed to overtaking their lives), there was still a need to tell them, and I got so many follow-up notes from survivors and their loved ones thanking me for listening. Our personal stories help us make sense of who we are, where we've been, and who we are becoming.

> *I lived three blocks south of the World Trade Center on 9/11. I thought at first an atomic bomb had hit.... Our super was on the roof taking pictures when the second plane came in, and it came so low he had to lie down and flatten himself. He said he could see the faces in the plane window. They evacuated us, and I left my apartment with only my dog, cell phone, and date book, thinking I'd be back in a day or so. They put us on a boat and it was like Noah's ark with all the dogs, cats, and people. There was this dead silence and ash everywhere. I kept thinking, "They killed my home. They killed what I love...." I ended up staying with friends on the east side of Manhattan for three weeks, then going to a hotel. We talked and talked and talked. It still helps to talk about it now because each time I do, it seems further away and hurts a little less. As terrifying as the experience was, it changed my life for the better because it gave me the impetus to finally quit my job and move—which I had been putting off doing before 9/11.*

Many therapies for trauma are based on the idea that healing begins when we become willing to share our story with another person. Survivors, spouses, children, friends, and family all hold a chapter in the story of a trauma. When we paste the experiences together, we begin to see how the effects of trauma are complex and far-reaching. I tried to keep the effects of Michael's trauma and the residue of an emotionally abusive first marriage inside me by soothing myself with food. Others may numb feelings or deny their stories with alcohol or other drugs. An episode with bulimia should have been a huge hint that I had a need to "bring up" some pain and truths, but I am a slow learner. It wasn't until years later, when my current therapist urged me to tell *my* trauma story, that I realized the value and necessity of such an endeavor.

To whom have you told *your* story of how you have been affected by your loved one's trauma? If you haven't discussed these things with anyone, ask yourself who could listen to your feelings, your confusion, your pain, and even your anger without judgment or advice? It is just as important to identify those people who might dismiss your experience or silence you by telling you to "just get over it."

> *My husband survived and his wounds healed, but the bombing was a life-changing event for us. We were so connected to the building and the people who worked there. Afterwards, a lot of good folks with good intentions said, "Now you just need to move on." My response was, "We are moving on, but this happened and our lives are never going to be the same." Nearly in anger (which is tough for me) I said, "If we just say it's over so move on, are we really respecting those lives that were lost?"*

People in recovery from a variety of addictions are often reminded, "We're as sick as our secrets," but it is often difficult to talk about things that may have been buried for years.

> *My son was sexually abused when he was a little boy, but he didn't tell anyone about it until he was an adult. It breaks my heart that I didn't know, and it explains so much about all the trouble he had growing up—including a couple of suicide attempts. I tried to talk about it to my brother, but he dismissed me, telling me it's in the past and that I needed to forgive the perpetrator (a relative). I got angry and told him that forgiveness*

was God's job, not mine. I feel so guilty that I wasn't there for my
son and wish I could talk about those feelings.

Choosing a respectful listener is an important part of telling our story. There will be times when our traumatized loved one might be the one to whom we express our feelings. There may also be times when he or she is emotionally unavailable and unable to listen attentively— just as there are times when we might not be the best listeners. I made the mistake of thinking I couldn't or shouldn't bother Michael with my problems or feelings when he was diagnosed with PTSD, but I learned I was wrong. When we both got healthier and learned to communicate more honestly, he told me it was important for him to feel needed and capable of giving support. "You know," he said, "PTSD is a disorder, not a cop-out. I want to be here for you too."

When a trauma is fresh, or the effects of a past trauma are first being realized, it may be wiser for you to express your feelings to someone other than your loved one and wait until the ground for mutual communication is a bit more solid. Asking an already emotionally-overburdened trauma survivor to listen to how their traumatic symptoms impact others while they're still reeling from trauma's initial blow could add to their guilt, anger, grief, depression, and shame, causing them to respond defensively or become even more distant. Of course, this will vary from trauma to trauma and individual to individual.

There may be times when you are feeling put out or put upon by your loved one's trauma-related behavior. At those times, it often helps to discuss those feelings with someone else first in order to clarify boundaries and take responsibility for your own actions and reactions.

....

HOW TO CHOOSE A GOOD LISTENER

- Be intentional when you think about who might be a good listener
- Consider confiding in someone you know who has also been affected by a loved one's trauma

- Observe prospective listeners in other situations to see how they handle themselves in a conversation
- Do they contribute honestly without pretending to have all the answers?
- Do they listen to others attentively without interrupting or taking over the conversation?
- Can you imagine being vulnerable with this person?
- Can this person keep a confidence?

Once you have a listener in mind, take a deep breath and ask them if they could set aside some time to talk with you. You might want to suggest a mellow coffee shop or other quiet place where you won't be interrupted. It helps if you can be specific in your request, perhaps saying something like, "Things have been a little tough for me as we all try to deal with what happened to Sue. I think it would really help me to talk about it. Would you have some time next week to listen?" Scheduling a specific time and place lets the other person know that this is important, and framing the question in this manner makes it clear what you are asking of that person.

Schedule long phone conversations ahead of time if your friend lives out of town. One of my closest friends lives 1,000 miles away. When one of us needs to have a heart-to-heart talk with the other, we'll call the other and first ask, "Is this a good time?" If it is, the one calling will then say, "Go draw a bath and call me back." Then we fill our respective tubs and can talk to each other without interruption from our quiet and warm long-distance cocoons.

If there is no one you can think of to whom you want to tell your story, you might want to find a good therapist or social worker who has expertise dealing with the primary and secondary effects of trauma. The best professional listeners serve as remarkable tour guides, helping you find your way through your pain and confusion.

It took me many years of practice and many classes in interpersonal communication to learn how to put feelings into words.

Identifying my feelings was tough enough; expressing them seemed unfathomable. I remember feeling paralyzed when a marriage counselor asked me what I was feeling. "Show me, then," he urged. "Stand up and show me where you are in this relationship." I moved in slow motion, got up, and walked to the farthest corner of the room, turned my back to my husband and the therapist, and covered my eyes with my hands. I am forever grateful that this insightful psychologist gave me a way to express myself when I could not find words to articulate my despair and loneliness. "Now come back and try to tell us how you feel." This simple exercise loosened me up, and the words began to flow with the tears.

Whoever you talk to, try not to worry about saying something perfectly. As those who have been through talk therapy can attest, one of the benefits of telling your story is the way things get clearer during the telling. You might not emerge from the experience with all the answers, but saying your feelings out loud and taking in feedback (both verbal and nonverbal) just might help you form a better idea of what you need to do next to take care of yourself.

CHOOSING A THERAPIST

There are many ways to find a therapist. A good place to start is to ask friends and family members if they know anyone they would recommend. However, be aware that even if they know someone they like, this therapist might not have expertise in trauma treatment. Give yourself permission to change therapists at any time if you do not feel the relationship is a good fit.

Here are some other ways to locate a therapist:

- Contact your local mental health agency or family physician.
- Contact your local state psychological association.
- If you or your spouse works for a large company or organization, check with the human resources or personnel office

to find out if the company provides mental health services or makes referrals.

- If you are a member of a Health Maintenance Organization (HMO), ask if mental health services are part of your coverage. If you have individual insurance, check your policy or call the company to see if these services are covered.
- The American Psychological Association has good "Find a Psychologist" information on its Web site: www.apa.org/ helpcenter/.
- Local mental health services are listed in the phone book in the blue Government pages. In the "County Government Offices" section for the county where you live, look for a "Health Services (Dept. of)" or "Department of Health Services" section. In that section, look for listings under "Mental Health." In the yellow pages, services and mental health professionals are listed under "counseling," "psychologists," "social workers," "psychotherapists," "social and human services," or "mental health." Health insurance may pay for mental health services, and some services are available at low cost according to your ability to pay.

Cyber Support

It is good—and it is essential—to interact with other people face-to-face, heart-to-heart, but it isn't always possible. Your friend may not be available when you need to talk; your loved one may be physically or emotionally unavailable; your therapist might not have any open appointments for a day or two; you may not be able to sleep and get out of bed at two a.m. yearning for a listening ear. At such times, consider an Internet forum for those who, like you, love a trauma survivor.

My wife has a rare kind of terminal cancer that is destroying her body and her mind. I found an Internet group for spouses and families of patients with the same disease and it has been a lifeline for me. My friends try to support me, but they can't know how difficult this is day-to-day. I don't have to explain myself to the online chat groups—they know what I'm going through because they're going through the same sorts of things.

Winnowing out the best and most informative sites can be a little tricky at first, but I've included some at the back of this book that you might find helpful. With the click of a mouse, you can be instantly connected to online support groups where you can get advice, compassion, and humor from others who are dealing with issues similar to your own. For example, www.ptsdforum.org has separate forums for those who deal with post-traumatic issues. Because, as written on the site, "Spouses and family are too often forgotten and often they receive all the worst that PTSD has to offer," the site includes a special forum for "carers." Here is a sample post from ptsdforum.org that will give you an idea of what to expect at such Internet sites:

I just really need some advice about caring for someone with PTSD. Can people with this illness really love somebody? I was a healthy, happy thirty-eight-year-old male living a good, stable life. I reconnected with an old girlfriend and we were very happy and really enjoying each other in a very positive way. We decided she should move in with me and start a life together. She mentioned in general conversation that she had PTSD from an abusive relationship but said she had dealt with it. In the last three weeks she has really gone into a shell. There's no sex anymore but we'll still hold hands and be close. She's very jumpy and isolated. She says she loves me so much and I tell her the same. She said she needs time to straighten things out and had to go back to see her mother. I think living with a man in a new relationship was just too much and triggered her into relapse. Thank you in advance to whoever responds to this thread. There have been some dark days, but I do see light at the end of the tunnel.

As caregivers dialogue with each other, they form connections, and a community of "cyber friends" grows. While a virtual community cannot—nor should it—take the place of live human interaction, the Internet can be a rich supplementary resource for those who have access to a computer and modem.

The Importance of Telling a Trauma Story

Telling our stories is only part of the equation. When we listen to each other with attentive ears and open and nonjudgmental hearts, the door to real intimacy opens even further. Our traumatized loved ones need to tell their stories too, and often it is us to whom they want to talk. However, this doesn't mean that we're ready to listen. Remember the analogy of the oxygen mask in the last chapter? Take care of yourself first. Garner the support and tools you need from friends, credible resources, or your therapist if you are feeling uncertain about your ability to be an attentive and compassionate listener because of your own emotional turmoil.

> *I got my husband back whole physically, and I think his heart is here too, but I'm not so sure about his mind. He still checks to see where his weapon is every time we get in a vehicle. Although his body is back, there is a war that remains between us. I am left to deal with the lost years of time, the lost love of my life. I want to talk with my husband about what he's going through, but I don't have the words. Hell, I don't even have the questions. What's the conversational opener to this: So you inadvertently killed Iraqi children. How's that going for you?*

As Catherall points out in *Back From the Brink*, "the first obstacle for you, the listener, to contend with is whether you really *do* want to know what your loved one's traumatic experience was like. Before you go any further, you need to examine whether you are indeed prepared to experience vicariously the awful emotions and details of your loved one's traumatization." You might first want to talk to someone who has experienced a similar trauma so you have a better idea of what your loved one might relate.

You might also be so angry with your loved one that attentive listening—at least for the time being—seems out of the question.

> *My husband has PTSD, and I've bent over backwards trying to support him. I gave up my good-paying job to relocate so he could pursue a "sure-fire" opportunity and dream. Then he lost his job because of a series of really bad business decisions on his part that put all we had worked for in jeopardy. I took a job at minimum wage to help out, but things turned into a real nightmare when the economy tanked. He couldn't find another position, and I found out he was buying things behind my back while I was struggling to pay bills so we wouldn't lose our house. We had already lost our health insurance. He came to me full of remorse, but I was just too mad and distrustful to listen.*

When Michael grew silent and uncommunicative, I'd often press him to talk about his feelings—a ridiculous endeavor when someone only "feels" numbness. At such times I'd walk away, rejected, lonely, and afraid. I'd blame myself for his detachment, and the "if onlies" would creep in: "If only I were thinner, prettier, smarter, more interesting. . ." Then we'd both bury ourselves in our respective work and the happy task of raising our daughter, pretending everything was fine. Eventually I learned that it requires time, distance, safety, trust, and courage for a trauma survivor to find words for what is so often unspeakable terror. Sometimes it's easier for survivors to relate their experiences to their therapists or another survivor before they talk to family or friends who may not understand or believe them.

> *I spent so much of my young life feeling dirty and disgusting that I became extremely watchful of everything so I wouldn't be exposed as this vile little girl who, for years, had "let" Uncle*

Bob have sex with her. I spent my childhood and especially my adolescence—when the abuse was going on—hiding everything about myself. My whole life was one big secret! I cry when I think of myself as that young girl and the daily terror of being exposed as a whore, when all the time it wasn't any of my doing at all. No wonder I used to fantasize about lying dead in a coffin and having my family crying because I was gone. Then I would finally get the attention I wanted.

I've met many men and women combat veterans who flat-out refuse to talk about their experiences with anyone but other veterans. There are many reasons for silence: guilt, shame, distrust, grief, and fear of being judged or disbelieved among them.

There are good reasons why we vets are hesitant to tell our stories except to each other. Too often we said to those who might have heard our stories, "If you weren't there, you won't understand." Can you blame us? Everyone has been flooded with the images and Hollywood stereotype of the crazed, baby-killing Vietnam veteran—the human powder keg—so why volunteer to be categorized that way when silence is an option? How can we explain the addictive life-and-death rush of combat—and, yes, of killing and surviving—if you haven't experienced it? How do we know you won't judge us?

Try not to feel hurt or rejected if your loved one is unable or unwilling to immediately talk with you about their trauma. The stories and feelings may come out a little at a time over time, so try to be patient and try not to force them to share before they are ready, as I so often did. It is healing—and I think essential—for survivors to talk to someone. If they seem distraught but silent, encourage them to talk to someone they can trust who can help them get the professional support they need. Even if they aren't ready to talk to you, your willingness to assist them in getting the help they need might speak volumes and pave the way for future conversations when both of you are ready to talk and to be heard.

Listening with the Ear in Your Heart

In *Storycatcher,* Baldwin points out how the word *heart* has within it the word *ear*. Attentive listening is an art we can practice so when our traumatized loved one *is* ready to talk, we can listen with open heart, open mind, *and* open ears. This is not a simple task. It isn't easy to be an active listener in today's world filled with so much noise, so many distractions, and too much to do. Instead of emptying our minds so we can really *hear* what someone is saying, we are often so eager to get our point across that we don't really pay attention to the speaker.

Deep listening can be transformational. It conveys respect and can empower a speaker by boosting self-esteem. When we listen attentively to someone, we convey the message, "This is important; *you* are important." An adult who listens respectfully makes a better employer, coworker, spouse, parent, and friend. A child who is listened to attentively is more likely to share things with a parent. And it's an honor for listeners when someone trusts you enough to share their thoughts and feelings.

> *My husband didn't want anything to do with me or the family. I kept asking him if I had done something, but he'd just sulk off. Things finally got so bad he went to see a therapist who deals with PTSD. Part of his "desensitization" homework was to tell me some things that had happened to him. He told me some of his nightmares and experiences, and it was such a relief to have him finally open up and to know that I wasn't causing what was going on with him. Little by little he's showing more emotion now, and I get glimpses of the guy I married. He actually cried the last time we talked.*

We may think we're good listeners, but most of us are usually more interested in our own thoughts and words, or too distracted with our own interests or concerns, to listen deeply to someone else.

We all know how it feels *not* to be listened to—when we're in the middle of telling a story and a listener looks away, or gets up to get a beverage in the middle of our sentence, or interrupts us with their story or to make a point or argue.

> *I went to see a therapist, but it seemed like she was more interested in telling her story than listening to mine. She talked about her recent surgery and discomfort, then turned her back to me while she took notes on her computer. It wasn't until the last third of the session that I finally got to speak.*

Being *really* listened to is a wonderful experience. When we feel heard, we feel cared for and respected. Our self-esteem and self-confidence grow, and our relationships usually improve. Attentive listening is a skill we can all hone. Active listeners learn to

- Suspend lecturing
- Squash the desire to talk about themselves or their experiences
- Avoid downplaying a speaker's concerns

Try the following active listening strategies when your loved one is ready to talk and you are ready to listen:

- Give your loved one your full attention by focusing on them and what they are saying. Turn off the television, the radio, and your computer, and turn toward the speaker so you can observe their body language. Be honest about your time. If you are really in the middle of something that cannot be interrupted, apologize and schedule a time when you can ensure your full attention and focus.
- Show you are listening by asking for clarification when needed, by making eye contact, and by adding an occasional "uh-huh," "I see," or nodding your head. Listening

isn't only done with the ears; our body language, posture, and level of attentiveness all say something about our interest and concern.

- Show that you understand by occasionally restating (paraphrasing) what the other person has said by asking things like "Are you saying such and such?" or saying "What I heard you say is . . ."

- Try to listen without judgment and resist the urge to interject your opinion. Be aware of your personal triggers or filters—things that, because of your personal experiences or history, might cause you to react with horror, anger, or fear. If a powerful emotion arises that distracts you momentarily, it's okay to apologize to your loved one with something like, "I'm sorry. That part of your story struck an emotional chord for me that took me away for a second. Could you repeat your last sentence? I really want to hear what you have to say." Be honest if you need a break by saying something like, "I'm really glad you're telling me about your experience, but this is difficult for both of us, and I'm feeling a bit overwhelmed. Could we do this again tomorrow?"

- Resist saying, "I know how you feel," but instead let your loved one know that you want to know what it was like and how it is for them to live with their trauma now.

- Make room for silence and give the speaker time to gather thoughts. It's fine to ask if they're done speaking before you respond.

- Don't give advice or diminish the speaker's experience or reactions. Validate feelings by saying something like "That must have been difficult," or "That sounds really frightening."

Finally, it's important to know when to back off. Pay attention to your loved one's body language as well as their words. If they seem agitated or emotionally overwhelmed, check in with them by asking how they're doing or if a break would be helpful. When Michael first talked about his trauma, decades before his PTSD diagnosis, he did so like a reporter, giving me facts but not feelings. The feelings came later and caught both of us by surprise. Sometimes, being there for each other simply meant holding each other and crying for what each of us had lost.

When It's Your Turn

Remember this goes both ways. It takes time, distance, safety, trust, patience, and courage for you to talk to your loved one about how the trauma has changed things for you. Give yourself the same permission you give your loved one—to talk when you are ready, to be silent when you need to be. Ideally, you will have moments of connection with your loved one in which you can *both* be honest about how trauma has affected each of you. Such moments can foster healing and intimacy if both of you are feeling strong and safe enough to speak and listen from your hearts.

As I said earlier, there is a time to listen and a time to talk. Expressing your feelings to each other is an imperfect process, but a worthwhile one if you hang in there, and use and share the listening skills you've gathered. You'll probably be able to tell by your loved one's body language or attitude if the time is right for them to listen to your feelings attentively without their getting too defensive, combative, distant, or controlling. It's also fine to simply ask them if it's a good time for them to listen to your feelings.

If you've practiced listening attentively to your loved one, you've already modeled this process, so they'll already know how good it feels to be listened to respectfully. Sometimes, subliminal lessons go a long way, but try not to give up if your loved one doesn't automatically get how to listen deeply. Reciprocal listening takes time and practice.

When I came across the *Could You Just Listen* piece (see sidebar), I shared it with Michael and we talked about the listening process and what it meant to be an attentive listener. I told him how hesitant I was to talk about my fears and feelings regarding his trauma and symptoms because I was afraid that I'd hurt his feelings or that he'd think I was being critical or whining. This conversation about listening opened the door for me to be able to tell him my difficult truths while he "just listened."

Consider making a copy of these tips and putting them on the refrigerator or bedroom wall as a reminder to listen to each other attentively.

....

COULD YOU JUST LISTEN?

When I ask you to listen to me and you start giving me advice, you have not done what I asked.

When I ask you to listen to me and you begin to tell me why I shouldn't feel that way, you are trampling on my feelings.

When I ask you to listen to me and you feel you have to do something to solve my problem, you have failed me, strange as that may seem.

Listen! All I asked was that you listen, not talk or do—just hear me.

When you accept as a simple fact that I do feel what I feel, no matter how irrational, then I can quit trying to convince you and can get about the business of understanding what's behind this irrational feeling.

Perhaps that's why prayer works, sometimes, for some people—because God is mute, and He/She doesn't give advice or try to fix things.

So, please listen and just hear me.

And if you want to talk, wait a minute for your turn, and I'll listen to you.

—Author unknown (adapted)

....

From Monologues to Dialogue

Telling your story and listening to your loved one's story is a great beginning, but these endeavors are *not* dialogue; dialogue is not two monologues pasted together. Listening to a loved one's trauma story is important, but it's equally important to know that you are heard when it is your turn to talk about your feelings.

Dialogue is the ability to hear and respond to what is being said. Dialogue is an act that lets your comments freely associate from one thought to the next, tracking with each other, moving through topics, and noticing those ideas that are of interest to one or the other of you. Practicing dialogue is like building a house. A foundation is laid and the participants both take turns building upon it.

Balanced communication begins when both parties practice the listening skills we've already discussed. As the Greek philosopher Epictetus wrote, "We have two ears and one mouth so that we can listen twice as much as we speak." Consider practicing balanced communication with a friend, a relative, or your loved one by setting a timer for ten minutes and taking turns talking while the other person listens attentively. The listener does not jump in at any time to comment or reply, but listens respectfully while the speaker talks without interruption. Was it more difficult for you to listen attentively or to talk without interruption? This exercise is a good start to talking with your loved one about feelings.

> *When I was going through therapy, I worked up the courage to call my siblings and tell them about my trauma. They listened carefully and then they talked and I listened. Their stories filled in the gaps in my memories, and I discovered that I wasn't the only one who remembered growing up in a house full of fear of our parents. I wasn't the only one who was too afraid to confront them. Our parents raised us kids with rules to deal with our troubles: Don't cry, don't talk, don't ask, don't get angry, don't be sad, stuff it, buck up, move on and get back to work, others have it worse, offer it up to Jesus (who suffered so much*

more), don't tell (family secrets). So here we are now as adults who have developed a range of unhealthy behaviors and techniques to deal with our pasts. We learned our lessons well, and we all learned not to feel. It felt so good to talk about it with them—at last.

What you think about something is very different from how you feel about it, and if both of you stick to "I" messages, the chances are better that you'll avoid blaming the other for your reactions. Try to say "I feel . . ." instead of "I feel that . . ." because when you use "that," it's easier to start talking about what you think instead of how you feel. It also helps to be as specific as you can be about your feelings. For example, "I feel a little irritated" isn't the same as "I feel very angry."

If you are bothered by your loved one's behavior, try to describe the specific behavior you don't like, then your feelings about it. Now that Michael and I are more aware of our past communication problems, our conversation today might look something like this:

Me: I'm really glad that you are finally talking about your trauma, but sometimes I feel a little lonely or ignored with so much of the focus on Vietnam.

Michael: I guess I do get carried away sometimes, but you invited me to run my thoughts and writing by you any time. Sometimes I feel confused because it seems like I'm getting mixed messages.

Me: What do you think we could do to balance things out better?

Michael: Maybe we could try to set aside time each day and take turns telling each other how we're doing and what's on our minds.

INTERNAL DIALOGUE

The next time you're feeling down or "stuck," try writing out a conversation. I first learned the technique of dialoguing with myself many years ago in a writing class. The instructor had us "talk back" to our internal censor—that little guy who sits on our shoulder hissing in our ear about how worthless we are. First I let him talk, and then I responded. It felt freeing to take him on, to defend myself on the page.

Having a conversation with yourself on the page can be an effective way to interrupt the stream of negative and distorted thoughts that may run through your mind when you feel in conflict, despair, or overcome with self-doubt. When you tell yourself things like "I am such a lousy partner," your softer, more rational self can recount the times you've stayed up late listening to your loved one; the little extras you do to contribute to a smooth-running household, the tender night your family shared last week relaxing and laughing together.

Practice dialogue by having a "conversation" on the page, taking the part of both speakers. Begin by stating something in your voice, then let the other person respond. Continue in this back-and-forth manner and see what happens.

One of my internal dialogues might go like this:

Critical Self: I never do anything right.

Softer Self: That's silly. You do lots of things right. Just today you remembered to send your friend a card, you met a deadline, and you helped an elderly woman find her car.

Critical Self: I'm lazy, and my house is always a mess. All my friends exercise, work, and keep their houses immaculate.

Softer Self: You were up until two a.m. working, and got up to do laundry at eight before you left. Maybe you can find time for a nap or a walk later. I think your friends feel overwhelmed too. Don't you remember S. telling you how she threw all her clutter in her closet when the doorbell rang?

Critical Self: I never follow through. I planned to clean last night, then my husband suggested we go out for dinner.

Softer Self: That sounds like fun. You'd been sad that you haven't had any time alone together lately. Sounds like a good choice to me. Would you rather have been cleaning?

Critical Self: No, you're right. It was a special night. I guess vacuuming can wait.

Well, you get the idea. When you dialogue with yourself, your more rational self usually quiets your distorted thoughts. You might also try writing out a conversation with another person.

Let your loved one "speak" to you on the page when you are angry or confused about their behavior; let your friend who hurt you "explain" their actions. I've even had a "conversation" with my late mother asking for her wise counsel and imagining her responses. I've also dialogued on paper with our favorite dog before we put her down, and even with my body. In every instance, it helped me see another point of view or accept a situation or a loss. In the case of my body, the exercise helped me appreciate that although I dislike certain aspects of it, it serves me well.

Of course, I know it is really me who holds the answers, but these dialogues help me correct my perspective and gain a clearer understanding of others in the process. They help me realize that I know more than I think I do.

CHAPTER 5

Self-Care III:
Declaring a "Toxic-Free" Zone

A wise elder told his grandson, "I feel as if I have two
wolves fighting in my heart. One wolf is angry, vengeful,
violent, arrogant, and resentful, filled with self-pity, false
pride, lies, greed, hate, and regret. The other wolf is loving,
compassionate, and generous, filled with humility, truth, joy,
hope, and peace. The same fight is going on in you—and in
every other person too."

The grandson thought for a moment, then asked,
"Which wolf will win?"

The grandfather answered, "The one you feed."

—NATIVE AMERICAN STORY

SOMETIMES IT IS THE WISE GRANDPARENT who teaches the lessons of balance and boundaries. Author Robert Fulghum writes
that we learn how to live and what to do in kindergarten, where
we are taught to play fair, share, take naps, hold hands, and stick
together. I continue to learn from my daughter and son-in-law,
who have established a haven of love and respect for their little
family and all who visit them.

On their wall is posted the rules of the household that all
four of them consistently follow: "Listen the first time. Use your

hands and words respectfully. No hitting or talking back. Clean up when it's time." When one of their twin toddlers gets angry or acts up, they never shout at them to stop. Instead, they empathize, saying something like, "I *know* you like to go outside and play with your trucks. That's a fun thing to do, but it's time for lunch, then naptime." And if misbehavior warrants a timeout, they always conclude it by making sure the child understands the reason for being disciplined.

At their house and in their relationships, feelings are not ignored; they're respected and dealt with when they arise. Michael and I are not let off the hook if we make a thinly veiled remark to Jessica or her husband that hints at displeasure, anger, or judgment. "You sound a little angry," "You look a little disgusted," Jessica or our son-in-law might note in one of our phone or in-person conversations. "Do you disapprove or disagree with what I said or did?" While it's often uncomfortable and requires a certain amount of emotional energy to have to clarify an action or reaction (especially when I *am* a little miffed about something), this practice of theirs defuses tension and prevents annoyances from growing into major grievances.

When a loved one suffers from a traumatic experience, raw and painful feelings—theirs *and* ours—rush to the surface or are buried deep. So many post-traumatic feelings like grief, hate, guilt, fear, hopelessness, helplessness, and shame, mutate into anger. Turned inward, anger can implode as depression or manifest in addictive behavior. Turned outward, anger can explode as rage.

> *I am a long-term survivor of childhood emotional abuse and neglect. My father committed suicide with a gun, and my best friend was killed in a bicycle accident. I am also married to a twenty-year NYC police officer who was shot and forced to kill another person. In addition, he lost half his unit at the World Trade Center attack, then had to search through the rubble for the remains of fallen others. I struggle with depression and my husband struggles with rage—which almost caused us to split up. Now I see a trauma specialist and my husband is getting help*

too. Initially, his rage and abuse triggered my symptoms, but he no longer does that and when I cry or get withdrawn he holds me, reassures me, and gets me to my therapist. Now we know we need to make our home environment a place of peace at all costs. Now it is an anchor for him too and a place where he can relax and unwind.

In the introduction to this book, I wrote that *trauma* comes from the Greek word for *wound.* When wounds aren't taken care of properly, they fester and get infected. Like wounds, our feelings about our loved one's trauma can become toxic if we don't tend to them. As scary as it may seem, we need to feel all of our feelings, just as our loved one needs to feel all of their feelings. Our mutual healing and our future serenity depend on it. Declaring a "toxic-free zone" doesn't mean establishing a sanctuary where only warm and fuzzy emotions are allowed. It means honoring ourselves and respecting others as complete human beings, made up of a wide range of complex and diverse feelings—some of which *are* warm and loving, others of which are dark and sometimes frightening.

Trauma and Anger

As the National Center for PTSD points out on its Web site, anger is often a central feature of a response to trauma because it is a core component of the survival response in humans. Anger helps us cope with life's difficulties by providing us with increased energy to persist in the face of obstacles. However, unmanaged or stifled anger can lead to a continued sense of being out of control, creating multiple problems in the lives of trauma survivors and those who love them.

My rage was off the charts when my little sister got raped. I just wanted to hunt down the bastard who did this to her, even though we didn't have a clue who he was. I was supposed to be her big brother protector, and I felt like I let her down. Finally, Mom took

me aside and told me that all my yelling wasn't helping anything—
that my sis needed hugs and reassurance, not a revenge-filled brother
who they all worried would do something crazy.

In her book, *Vietnam Wives,* Aphrodite Matsakis, Ph.D., stresses the importance of getting in touch with your anger and learning how to deal with it in a constructive rather than destructive way. "Many of the women suffer from impacted anger just as do their partners," she writes. "If a woman has repressed her anger over time regarding a series of incidents, then each new conflict with her partner brings to the surface not only the anger appropriate to that particular incident, but all the built-up angers from the past." Meanwhile, Matsakis writes, many traumatized loved ones fear hurting their spouses or children if they let their anger show and they can't control it, so they shut down emotionally or try to dull their feelings with alcohol or other drugs. Others turn to food.

I found it interesting and a little sad when I read in Matsakis' book that 20 percent of the wives of PTSD patients polled at vet centers were significantly overweight—some of them double their ideal weight. "It is possible that these women literally swallowed their anger as well as other feelings," she writes. One of the wives she counseled, for example, binged whenever her husband disappointed or ridiculed her or cheated on her with other women. "Each of his blondes has cost me thirty pounds," she told Matsakis. While it may appear that this type of "revenge eating" is meant to punish a spouse, Matsakis writes that on a deeper level it is a form of self-abuse that results in low self-esteem. In such instances, the partner of a spouse with PTSD doesn't even feel entitled to their anger.

Suppressed anger has a way of seeping out in other unhealthy ways when our emotional "cup" gets to the point of overflowing. I remember shouting at a mother at a park for letting her young child litter. Rather than thinking she may not have even seen the minor infraction, I marched over to her with the discarded wrapper and waved it in her face, yelling, "Can't you teach your kid not to litter?"

I've also been known to give the finger to bad drivers. Others who stuff their anger relate similar stories.

> *About a year ago, I just started getting very angry very quickly. Road rage would come so easily that I was afraid to drive. I would be very easily irritated by coworkers. And I never could seem to direct it properly or find a cause for it. I wanted to scream. I did anger-releasing rituals, grounding exercises, all to some relief but all too temporary. Now I'm beginning to connect the rage to our family's trauma and slowly, slowly I think I'm being healed. [Sometimes] the only way out is through.*

Research also reveals that anger can be a normal response to betrayal or the loss of trust, particularly in situations of interpersonal exploitation or violence. In situations of early childhood abuse, the trauma and shock of the abuse has been shown to interfere with an individual's ability to regulate emotions.

> *This probably will sound strange, but I do not like to be angry. It could be grounded in my upbringing in church, or the way I have seen anger explode in family settings. Whatever the reasons are, I was raped repeatedly by a stranger at gunpoint at the age of twelve and molested by an uncle in early childhood. Should I be pissed? YES! But anger scares me. The pure rage is what hurt me. It is the instrument that slashed my soul, and so I am very reluctant to hold that sword of fury in my hands. I am afraid it will kill me or others.*

For a trauma survivor, angry or violent outbursts can be linked to hyperarousal symptoms (sleep problems and nightmares, irritability, difficulty concentrating, hypervigilance, and exaggerated responses). Trauma survivors—especially those whose symptoms go untreated— are frequently on edge, which can cause them to be easily provoked or even look for a "depository" (or rationale) for the rage that boils within them. This makes them particularly susceptible to things like bar fights or domestic violence, often putting their families and friends on constant alert, which ironically fuels their own suppressed anger.

> *My dad is a Vietnam vet with PTSD and war wounds. When he got home from the hospital, he went out drinking and some guy took his money off the bar. He told the guy he would be back and the money better be on the bar when he got there. He left to get a gun and returned to the bar with it, but shot his foot when he pulled it out. With all the meds he was on and the drinking, he didn't even know he shot himself.*

While aggression can be an appropriate behavior in certain threatening situations, the National Center for PTSD states on its Web site that those with post-traumatic symptoms can get stuck in an aggressive mode or become passive-aggressive (for example, complaining, backstabbing, deliberately being late, or purposely doing a poor job).

> *My husband's rage was so unpredictable. He'd be sweet one minute, then fly off the handle the next, threatening me or kicking our dog out of the way. After a rage attack, he'd either blame me for his anger and not talk for days, or he'd be so remorseful I thought he might hurt himself. My adult children finally took me aside and told me they were worried about my safety. I got help for myself but he refused to see anyone. We're separated now and will probably get divorced, but I just couldn't live like that anymore.*

Angry loved ones can also become self-aggressive, engaging in self-destructive activities, self-blame, being self-critical, or injuring themselves. As Matsakis illustrated, those closest to the trauma survivor can also exhibit these behaviors if they ignore or bury their true emotions.

So much about trauma is about the loss of control. We couldn't control what happened to our loved one, and we can't control how he or she deals with post-traumatic symptoms. Many trauma survivors also feel that their lives are spinning out of control. In an effort to maintain an illusion of control in the wake of trauma symptoms, some families get compulsively rigid about rules (be on time, sit up straight, make your bed, put it back where you found it) and blow up if those rules are not followed religiously.

Michael grew up in a household filled with rules where he learned to stifle all feelings, especially anger. Then he went to a Catholic seminary filled with more rules, then on to the Marine Corps and Vietnam, where following rules and adopting the typical soldiers' mantra, "it don't mean nothin'" kept him alive. By the time he reentered the world after Vietnam, the "don't feel" rule was so cemented into him that the thought of expressing anger terrified him. He had been sitting on feelings for so many years, he feared a volcanic eruption if he got in touch with his true emotions. So we limped along, with me often brimming over with misdirected emotion and Michael often lost in an emotional void.

Uncovering Uncomfortable Feelings

Although our feelings may seem to pounce from shadows and catch us unaware, our bodies can give us clues about tumultuous emotions— even if our minds are numb to them. Pay attention to that lump in your throat, your sweaty palms, your tense and aching shoulders, the knot in your stomach, the headache, or your racing heart. Remove yourself from an atmosphere of tension and go someplace where you can breathe deeply into the bodily sensation. Try to sit quietly or take a calm walk. Try to identify the corresponding emotion.

Hit your emotional "pause" button if you sense anger rising to the surface, and recall the previous discussion about cognitive distortions. Ask yourself, "What's the story behind the story?" Are you really angry with the rude clerk, or are you frustrated about something that happened with your loved one? Are you really that angry because your child didn't do their homework, or are you overcome and exhausted at having to handle so many responsibilities? Is your anger linked to a sense of helplessness or hopelessness? What's the deeper story?

I had a chance to attend a weeklong retreat with Vietnamese monk Thich Nhat Hahn, who talked a lot about anger. He said that anger is a shield for grief and described a cord that connects anger and grief back to a prior hurt. Rage is not a venting of anger but a way to further water the seeds of anger, which he said only leads to more sorrow. He taught me that I am my anger. I should own it, and embrace it with mindfulness and tenderness to gain understanding about its roots. I know now that so many of my powerful emotions about my loved one's trauma are made stronger because of my own childhood experiences. I've learned not to express or suppress anger, but to transform it by uncovering its true source. Thich Nhat Hahn said that when a baby cries, a parent doesn't stop the crying; they look for and then tend to the reason for the tears. He taught me that we need to "baby" our anger and treat it with the same love and understanding.

A former firefighter told me that first responders use the acronym H.O.T. (Hazardous Overload of Thoughts) as a way to describe what happens when the "emotional backdraft" from pent-up and ongoing trauma gets to be too much. This buildup of unexpressed feelings occurs among family and friends of trauma survivors too. Pay close attention to what's going on in your body. Is your emotional thermometer running too H.O.T?

Before your anger explodes into rage or implodes into self-loathing, stop and try to complete the sentence, "I feel _____." Sometimes it helps to name a feeling in writing and keep your pen to the paper, not stopping to edit yourself or your feelings. Identifying your feelings to yourself in this way is like extracting venom from a snakebite. You may still have to salve the wound, but it is no longer toxic. Some experts suggest limiting the amount of time you sit with your feelings. They also caution against doing too much self-examination of this sort at bedtime because it can interfere with much-needed sleep.

Releasing emotion through writing or through something physical like walking, running, breathing deeply, or getting a massage, also relieves the tension that is stored with the feeling. Once you have calmed your body and your emotions, you are better able to express them to a friend or your loved one without rage or blame.

I've tried to help my friend with his anger. He's got such a short fuse. He's trying to cope with his wife and her trauma symptoms and her complete dependency on him. Then they had a house fire and he's got all that to contend with. One day, I walked him out into the woods and said, "I bet you're so angry you could just scream," so we took turns screaming until we got hoarse. We both felt so much better; we just started laughing.

With time and practice, you will be able to greet the beginning of a feeling like anger as a familiar (though sometimes unwelcome) visitor. "Oh, there you are again. What are you hiding behind your back this time?"

Protecting Yourself from Another's Toxicity

When you are the primary support for a traumatized loved one, you deserve to be supported genuinely and loved unconditionally. You deserve to be listened to and treated respectfully—just as others deserve to be treated respectfully by you.

There is support, and there is sabotage, however. A supportive friend does not try to talk you out of your feelings or insinuate that you or your loved one should just move on or "get over" a traumatic experience. In fact, a truly supportive friend will not suggest what you *should* or *should not* do or feel in any circumstance.

If you are feeling uncertain about whether a particular friend is helping or hindering your own healing in the wake of your loved one's trauma, ask yourself if your friend listens without defining or judging who you are and what your problem is. In what ways do you feel accepted? In what ways do you feel judged? It's fine for a trusted friend to ask for clarification or urge you to go deeper into a feeling or reaction. It's not helpful, however, for a friend to attack or challenge your feelings in a way that feels more like combat than support.

> *I'm tired of my friend discounting the effects of my partner's trauma on me and my family and arguing that PTSD should not be seen as a disorder. I don't care what you want to call it, something claimed a part of her after the attack and changed our family in the process. We still see this friend socially, but no more serious conversations for a while.*

When warning bells go off in your mind or body during a conversation with a supposedly supportive friend, you may need to take a break from the relationship—at least until you are feeling less vulnerable or not so emotionally and physically exhausted. If you choose, you can thank the friend for their concern, but simply explain that you don't care to talk about the situation. There is no need to blame, punish, or lecture. If your friendship was a close one and you want to say more, remember to use "I" language and take responsibility for your own thoughts, feelings, and actions.

Things get a little trickier when your loved one is the one spewing venom and you find yourself in the line of fire. Trauma symptoms and PTSD are no excuse for your loved one to abuse, mistreat, threaten, or endanger you or your family. Leave the house immediately if you sense you or your children are in danger, and call for backup from the police, a crisis center, a neighbor, or a friend, depending on the severity of the situation.

In calmer times, try to develop some prevention strategies with your loved one so things don't escalate to a dangerous level. You might want to ask your loved one what helps and what doesn't help when he or she is feeling emotionally out of control.

> *Another thing I do when I feel rage building is tell whoever is around that I need to be left alone—completely alone. Then I usually curl up in a fetal position until I can feel safe again.*

Sometimes it takes a long time, but my boyfriend knows that I'm working on calming down. People with PTSD are extremely afraid. I think the key is to recognize when our "fight/flight" is kicking in and do anything at all to intercept it and go to a place where we can make ourselves feel safe again. I know for me, this means I can have no humans around me at all.

Once again, it comes down to balance, boundaries, and honest communication. If you and your loved one pay close and respectful attention to each other, you'll probably know when tension is mounting. If you've talked about it beforehand, you'll be able to say—without feeling selfish or rejected—"I need some space" or be able to ask "Do you want some space?" or "Do you want to call Jack or somebody to talk?" Giving yourselves time and space to cool H.O.T. feelings is a great exercise in self-care and healthy boundary setting.

In a toxic-free household, members also notice and express appreciation for the positive things that happen. Michael and I got in the habit of keeping a combined journal. We keep the book in a special place and when the spirit moves either of us, we jot down little notes for each other. This journal is also "toxic-free." We don't complain or shout on the pages; we express appreciation for something the other has done; we share an observation or thought; and sometimes we own a feeling or render an apology. We usually don't discuss our entries. For us, the journal is a reminder of what we love and appreciate about each other, and reading a sweet note from Michael is like getting a tender hug.

....

NEGOTIATING TOXIC-FREE RELATIONSHIPS

Years ago, a friend who was in recovery for alcohol and other drugs gave me a copy of the following "credo" as a blueprint for our own relationship. Hold the statements and intentions up to the mirror of your friendships and your relationship with your loved one to see if each relationship meets these standards. If you choose, share this credo with your friend or loved one as my friend shared it with me. Use it as a model or even a contract with that person. If you want, you can even make it official by signing a copy.

A Credo for My Relationships with Others

You and I are in a relationship which I value and want to keep. We are also two separate persons with our own individual values and needs.

So that we will better know and understand what each of us values and needs, let us always be open and honest in our communication.

When you are experiencing a problem in your life, I will try to listen with genuine acceptance and understanding in order to help you find your own solutions rather than imposing mine. And I want you to be a listener for me when I need to find solutions to my problems.

At those times when your behavior interferes with what I must do to get my own needs met, I will tell you openly and honestly how your behavior affects me, trusting that you respect my needs and feelings enough to try to change the behavior that is unacceptable to me. Also, whenever some behavior of mine is unacceptable to you, I hope you will tell me openly and honestly so I can try to change my behavior.

And when we experience conflicts in our relationship, let us agree to resolve each conflict without either of us resorting to the use of power to win at the expense of the other's losing. I respect your needs, but I also must respect my own. So let us always strive to search for a solution that will be acceptable to both of us. Your needs will be met, and so will mine—neither will lose, both will win.

In this way, you can continue to develop as a person through satisfying your needs, and so can I. Thus, ours can be a healthy relationship in which both of us can strive to become what we are capable of being. And we can continue to relate to each other with mutual respect, love, and peace.

—Dr. Thomas Gordon
(www.gordontraining.com/A_Credo_for_Your_
Relationships_with_Others.html)

CHAPTER 6

Trauma and Addiction: Weathering the Storms

Our storms bring to the surface the issues that plague us. . . .
Recovery is a whole series of storms, storms that help to sprout
new growth, storms that flush clean our own clogged drains.
The peace that comes after a storm is worth singing about.

Each storm can be likened to a rung on the ladder to
wholeness, the ladder to full membership in the healthy
human race. The storms make climbing tough, but we get
strength with each step. The next storm will be more easily
weathered.

—KAREN CASEY,
Each Day a New Beginning

HAVE A HEADACHE? TAKE AN ASPIRIN. Need to relax? Have a
drink or light up a joint. Need a diversion? Shop 'til you drop.
Can't sleep? Take a pill. We are a society of quick fixes, so it
should come as no surprise that an alarming number of people
affected by trauma try to numb their feelings with alcohol or
other drugs, or other unhealthy and compulsive behaviors.

*I have trouble sleeping because of my PTSD and nightmares,
so I've gotten into the habit of having a couple of drinks and*

puffs of marijuana every night. It's the only way I can relax and fight off the demons.

According to an article posted on the National Center for PTSD's Web site, 25 to 75 percent of those who have survived abusive or violent trauma also report problems with alcohol use. Also, 10 to 33 percent of survivors of accidental, illness-related, or disaster-related trauma report problematic alcohol use, especially if they are troubled by persistent health problems or pain. An alarming 60 to 80 percent of Vietnam veterans seeking PTSD treatment have alcohol use disorders. The National Institutes of Health reports on its Web site that several studies have also linked PTSD to nicotine dependence.

As troubling as those well-documented statistics are, they don't tell the whole story, because those numbers just deal with trauma survivors and their unhealthy relationship with alcohol and cigarettes. But what about other out-of-control behaviors? What about the families of trauma survivors? What about you? Do you try to numb the pain and confusion you feel about your loved one's trauma by eating or starving it away, drugging or drinking it away, gambling it away, exercising it away, working it away, or compulsively clicking it away by spending long hours on your computer?

Personal growth guru John Bradshaw in his book *Bradshaw on: The Family* defines addiction as "a pathological relationship to any mood-altering experience that has life-damaging consequences." Despite the danger of losing a job, a marriage and family, friendships, finances, health, or self-respect, addicted individuals continue their unhealthy behavior. Their actions may have masked or numbed their pain at first, but eventually they lose control and their compulsive behaviors become the source of additional pain.

I didn't realize it at first, but I started to exhibit some of the same post-traumatic behavior as my son who was diagnosed with PTSD. He tried to escape his feelings with alcohol. After his death, I started drinking excessively. I was numb and angry.

I was afraid to sleep because every time I closed my eyes, I'd see him hanging there. I hardly drank before, but all of a sudden I was spending a lot on whiskey and got us into a financial bind. I felt powerless.

While abuse of alcohol and other drugs is easier to spot, some compulsive behaviors are subtler and may even get excused or ignored in a society that encourages consumerism, applauds overachievers, values thinness, and embraces perfectionism. For many years, I viewed Michael's type A tendencies as admirable. Neither of us thought of them as coping techniques or connected them to his post-traumatic symptoms. Eventually, however, his workaholism became a point of real controversy. His job came first, and I often complained that I became the last thing on his list of priorities—if I made the list at all. When he was home, he attacked house projects with the same perfectionism he brought to the office. Our attempts to do projects together usually failed because I felt I could not perform to his standards. When he wasn't consumed by work or house maintenance, he exercised compulsively for marathons, triathlons, or hundred-mile bike rides.

Meanwhile, I compulsively poured my energy into the lives of my family and friends instead of tending to my own life. I tried to control Michael and his schedule, and I got overinvolved in Jessica's life—often smothering her instead of mothering her appropriately. I tried to be the perfect wife, mother, friend, and daughter and I expected reciprocal devotion from others. I was miserable. As they say in Twelve Step circles, an expectation is a premeditated resentment, and I was resentment personified. Dejected and lonely, I'd sometimes secretly soothe myself with food.

Michael's workaholic and my codependent behaviors almost destroyed our marriage, but we both got the help we needed. Once exposed to the light of day (and the light of our competent counselors), we were able to recognize our behaviors as unhealthy. We learned it is possible to binge on work, exercise, food, and relationships with the fervor of an alcoholic or drug addict. We also learned about the strong link between trauma and addictive behavior, and how Michael's compulsivity was his way to avoid painful memories and feelings. We learned how many of my own unhealthy actions were in response to his behavior and post-traumatic symptoms. It was a humbling epiphany.

It is common and understandable that survivors of trauma and those who love them may try to escape their pain, confusion, grief, anger, guilt, and fear with substances or behaviors that numb those upsetting feelings. They might even be successful in running away from their post-traumatic reality for a while. Michael and I both learned that we could not live in illusion forever. We learned that in order to heal, we *must* feel.

Common Characteristics of Addictive Behavior

As Ruth C. Engs, author of *Alcohol and Other Drugs: Self Responsibility*, emphasizes,

> A person can become addicted, dependent, or compulsively obsessed with anything. Some researchers imply that there are similarities between *physical addiction* to various chemicals, such as alcohol and heroin, and *psychological dependence* to activities such as compulsive gambling, sex, work, running, shopping, or eating disorders. It is thought that these behavior activities may produce beta-endorphins in the brain, which makes the person feel "high." Some experts suggest that if a person continues to engage in the activity to achieve this feeling of well-being and euphoria, he/she may get into an addictive cycle.

According to Engs, there are many common characteristics among various addictive behaviors:

- Obsession with the object, activity, or substance
- Continued engagement in the behavior even though it causes harm or problems

- Irritability, restlessness, depression, and a craving to pursue the activity when not engaged in the behavior
- Loss of control regarding the duration or intensity of the behavior (for example, drinking several beers when intending to drink one; eating an entire box of cookies; buying several pairs of shoes when shopping for a different item)
- Denial that there is a problem
- Secretiveness (for example, hiding receipts, lying about alcohol or other drug use, hiding emails or Web sites)
- Difficulty remembering details about the compulsive behavior (for example, being unable to recall how much money was lost gambling; experiencing blackouts; forgetting what was purchased)
- Low self-esteem

My husband had classic trauma symptoms. He was depressed and distant or he'd blow up over the littlest thing. It got to be this emotional roller coaster, and I'd get so sad and lonely. Although I have trouble spending money on myself, I discovered I felt great when I'd buy something special for friends or my grandkids. I loved their excitement and gratitude. It made me feel loved and special. But my spending got out of control and I'd take out a new credit card and transfer the balance when I tapped out an old account. Robbing Peter to pay Paul, I guess you'd call it. I paid the bills, so it was easy to hide it from my husband. Then I started stockpiling the gifts, hiding them in places my husband wouldn't look. Meanwhile, he got in therapy and got better, but by then I had gotten us in serious financial trouble.

Many Web sites offer self-tests for those who suspect they might be dependent on a particular substance or behavior, but these are only meant to inform—not diagnose. It is important that you consult a qualified professional for a full evaluation if you think you might have a substance abuse or compulsive behavior problem. Ideally, the therapist, doctor, mental health professional, or counselor you consult will have a good working knowledge of addictive behavior *and* the secondary effects of trauma.

Powerlessness is *Not* Helplessness—a Twelve Step Recovery Primer

Those who love a trauma survivor—whether the survivor is a friend, spouse, parent, or child—know something about powerlessness. In previous chapters, I discussed how we did not have the power to control what happened to our loved ones, and we do not have the power to control how (or whether) they deal with the aftermath of their trauma. The sense of powerlessness we already feel with regard to our traumatized loved one grows dramatically if we begin to abuse alcohol or other drugs, or if we adopt compulsive behaviors in an effort to cope with the spillover effects of another's trauma.

> *When my girlfriend withdrew emotionally and physically after the rape, I started visiting porn sites on the Internet—just out of curiosity, I told myself. Then I started posting things in different sex chat rooms. I'd do this late at night after she was asleep. It became an obsession. I didn't sleep, so I was worthless at work and I was no help to my girlfriend. When she finally did turn to me for support, I was the one who wasn't there.*

It makes sense that the first of the Twelve Steps of recovery from addictive behavior deals with the admission of powerlessness. Until we acknowledge that we have a dependency problem, we cannot begin to deal with it. So many of us who are the primary support person for a traumatized loved one know what it feels like to have our lives spin out of control. Add addictive behavior to the mix, and our lives can become unmanageable—the other part of the First Step.

> *The stress of dealing with his trauma became overwhelming and I developed a dependence on alcohol. After a night of soli-*

tary drinking I had a hangover the next morning, looked in the mirror, and didn't like what I saw. Drinking numbed me for a while, but eventually alcohol unleashed all my pent-up feelings and caused me to lose emotional control.

If you are struggling with dependency problems of your own, you might want to try working the Twelve Steps that were carved out for alcoholics in 1935, then adapted for hundreds of other addictive and compulsive behaviors. In over twenty years of writing about addiction and recovery, I've had the privilege to meet and interview hundreds of recovering people who have applied the lessons and practices of the Twelve Steps to turn their lives around. I find the Steps to be such practical tools; such logical suggestions for taking care of oneself and assuming responsibility for one's own actions and reactions. And the "take what you want and leave the rest" approach in Twelve Step recovery provides enough room to use the principles and suggestions that work best in each individual situation.

Once we admit that our lives have become unmanageable (Step One), we stop trying to control everything and everyone and begin to trust that things will work out if we get out of our own way. We've been like children who put their fingers into a Chinese finger puzzle. The more they pull, trying to release their two index fingers from the webbed tube, the tighter the hold. Finally, they discover that all they have to do is let go, and the tube will slacken enough to let their fingers easily slide free. To me, this is the essence of Step Two and what people in recovery mean when they talk about letting go.

Letting go does not mean giving up. We've tried white-knuckling our way out of chaos, and it didn't work. Step Three reminds us about the importance of accepting help from an outside source—which can be a mutual-help group, a therapist, God, or something else we've defined as a "Higher Power."

I am spiritual but not religious, so I was put off at first by the mention of God when I first read the Steps. Then an agnostic friend who had been in a recovery group for decades explained that Twelve Step philosophy is about transformation, not religion, and that in Twelve Step groups, "God" or "Higher Power" can be the gentler part of yourself, or any loving thing, group, or entity outside yourself that gives you comfort or a focus for meditation. No belief in the supernatural is required. My friend explained, "In group, they say to think of G.O.D. as an acronym that means 'good orderly direction.' They also say the Steps work for people who believe in God and for those who don't believe in God—but they *never* work for people who think they *are* God. Nature is my Higher Power. My friend who practices Zen meditation chose Buddha." His comments brought to mind a saying I came across at a Franciscan mission, "I do not want a God who is limited by my imagination."

Steps Four through Nine are about taking an honest and thorough look at ourselves to find out, then deal with, the personal roadblocks we erect that keep us in the throes of our addictive behaviors. We also acknowledge our strengths. In Twelve Step jargon, this process is called "taking a searching and fearless inventory." This is like a business owner who inventories their stock to see which products are usable, which are damaged, and which are unsalable. When we take a personal inventory, we identify the characteristics, behaviors, and distorted thoughts that feed our addictive behavior, then work to get rid of them as we strengthen and expand our positive characteristics. We also list the people who may have been hurt by our addictive behavior—including ourselves. Then we share our list with another person and make amends to the people we've harmed (unless doing so would cause further harm).

Taking a personal inventory helps us accept our role in various life events, but it also relieves us of any shame or misplaced guilt we may be carrying for things that were not our fault or responsibility. When we work Steps Four through Nine, we begin to clear out the debris of the past and garner strength and courage for a more honest and richer present. We become "teachable." These steps are not dictates, only suggestions that you might want to try. They offer a way to release dishonesty, fear, and resentment, and only ask that you have a *willingness* to change and let go of unhealthy behavior and attitudes.

It is said that Twelve Step recovery is a process—not an event. We don't work the Steps one time and set them aside; they are valuable booster shots that help keep us healthy and sane, and we can go back to them at any time. I think of Steps Ten and Eleven as maintenance Steps—reminders to keep taking your inventory and acknowledging your mistakes as you continue to ask for guidance and admit your limitations.

Finally, I see Step Twelve as an encouragement to seek out a supportive community where you share and practice the lessons and joy of recovery. To me, the "spiritual awakening" in Step Twelve refers to the internal change that makes recovery from compulsive behavior possible. A Twelve Step group is the great leveler; a place where individuals who may differ in every other area of their lives come together because of the one thing they do share—addiction.

> *In twenty years of AA, I've never once experienced antagonism because of personal differences. The only arguments I've witnessed aren't because someone is rich or poor or black or white; they're because someone isn't being truthful to themselves or to the group about their addiction. You don't come to a mutual-help meeting as a Republican or a Democrat or a millionaire or a bum; you come as someone who is trying to stay clean and sober. You're no better and you're no worse than the person sitting next to you, but you're all better for being there and for trying.*

Twelve Step groups are not therapy groups or pity parties. The most effective groups are action groups were members share how the Steps are helping them make positive changes in their lives. The healthiest groups are those in which members listen to each other without interruption, and squelch the need or desire to advise, criticize, or judge another member. Anonymity and confidentiality are respected, and members are told that, "what is said in the room, stays in the room." You may want to check out www.12step.org or www .addictionsandrecovery.org for more information about addiction, recovery, and various Twelve Step groups.

The Twelve Steps are one recovery approach that has worked for many people throughout the world, but there are other paths to recovery that might seem a better fit for you. The important thing is that you take action and get the help and support you need if a compulsive behavior or dependency on alcohol or other drugs is increasingly affecting your life. Whatever approach you choose— meditation, Twelve Step, or other mutual-help groups—it should not preclude individual therapy if you need or feel you could benefit from one-on-one counseling. Even Bill W., the founder of AA, sought psychotherapy for his depression. The effects of your loved one's trauma can be deep and life-altering and all the more complex if you also struggle with an out-of-control behavior. Seek and accept all the help you need.

....

THE TWELVE STEPS OF ALCOHOLICS ANONYMOUS AND AL-ANON

(Bold italics added)

1. We admitted we were powerless over alcohol *(or food, or gambling, or debt, or trauma, etc.)*—that our lives had become unmanageable.
2. Came to believe that a Power greater than ourselves could restore us to sanity.
3. Made a decision to turn our will and our lives over to the care of God *as we understood Him.*
4. Made a searching and fearless moral inventory of ourselves.
5. Admitted to God, to ourselves, and to another human being the exact nature of our wrongs.
6. Were entirely ready to have God remove all these defects of character.
7. Humbly asked Him to remove our shortcomings.

8. Made a list of all persons we had harmed, and became willing to make amends to them all.
9. Made direct amends to such people wherever possible, except when to do so would injure them or others.
10. Continued to take personal inventory and when we were wrong promptly admitted it.
11. Sought through prayer and meditation to improve our conscious contact with God *as we understood Him*, praying only for knowledge of His will for us and the power to carry that out.
12. Having had a spiritual awakening as the result of these steps, we tried to carry this message to alcoholics *(participate in a recovery group of some type)*, and to practice these principles in all our affairs.

The Twelve Steps of AA are taken from *Alcoholics Anonymous,* 4th ed. (New York: Alcoholics Anonymous World Services, 2001), 59–60.

Some recovering people draw great strength and support from a Twelve Step fellowship, but find it easier to work the Steps if they change the "God language" to more comfortably reflect their personal beliefs. Here is a version of the Twelve Steps written by Bodhi, of Sydney, Australia.

THE TWELVE STEPS FOR NON THEISTS

1. We admitted our addictive craving over alcohol *(or food, or gambling, or debt, or trauma, etc.)* and recognized its consequences in our lives.
2. Came to believe that a power other than self could restore us to wholeness.
3. Made a decision to go for refuge to this other power as we understood it.
4. Made a searching and fearless moral inventory of ourselves.

5. Admitted to ourselves and another human being the exact moral nature of our past.
6. Became entirely ready to work at transforming ourselves.
7. With the assistance of others and our own firm resolve, we transformed unskillful aspects of ourselves and cultivated positive ones.
8. Made a list of all persons we had harmed.
9. Made direct amends to such people where possible, except when to do so would injure them or others. In addition, made a conscientious effort to forgive all those who harmed us.
10. Continue to maintain awareness of our actions and motives, and when we acted unskillfully promptly admitted it.
11. Engaged through the practice of meditation to improve our conscious contact with our true selves, and seeking that beyond self. Also used prayer as a means to cultivate positive attitudes and states of mind.
12. Having gained spiritual insight as a result of these steps, we practice these principles in all areas of our lives, and make this message available to others in need of recovery.

....

Double Trouble: Trauma Survivors and Addiction

Addiction and post-traumatic symptoms often go hand in hand. Your caregiving burden is made all the more difficult if your loved one (or you or other family members) is self-medicating with alcohol or other drugs. Substance abuse only makes post-traumatic symptoms worse. Although alcohol and other drugs can provide a *temporary* feeling of distraction and relief, they also reduce your ability to concentrate, enjoy life, and be productive. Substance use and abuse can also increase emotional numbing, social isolation, anger and irritability, depression, and the feeling of needing to be on guard (hypervigilance). Already impaired sleep can become more disturbed, making it all the more difficult to cope with trauma memories and stress.

Alcohol or other drug use reduces the effectiveness of post-traumatic treatment, and substance use problems can lead to other mental or physical problems. According to the National Center for PTSD Web site, as many as 10 to 50 percent of adults with alcohol use disorders and PTSD also have one or more of the following serious disorders:

- Anxiety disorders (such as panic attacks, phobias, incapacitating worry, or compulsions)
- Mood disorders (such as depression)
- Disruptive behavior disorders (such as attention deficit or antisocial personality disorder)
- Addictive disorders (such as addiction to or abuse of alcohol or street or prescription drugs)
- Chronic physical illness (such as diabetes, heart disease, or liver disease)
- Chronic physical pain due to physical injury or illness or due to no clear physical cause

Substance abuse is called a family disease because its effects are far-reaching. Relationships become even more strained and distant; financial problems mount, conflicts become even more frequent and severe; and everyone affected becomes more vulnerable to domestic violence brought about by a loved one's rage and out-of-control behavior.

I was wounded in Vietnam and spent nine months in a hospital because of my wounds. I sought help in 1977 because of anxiety, but that was before they knew much about PTSD. About four years ago, my drinking got so bad my daughter told me she felt like she only had one parent—even though I was physically there. It shook me up. Now I go to three AA meetings a week. My wife and daughter went through family week with me, which helped all of us, and our relationship is better than it ever has

been because I no longer feel the need to fight. I can let things go.
I've even gotten smarter at work somehow!

When a trauma survivor with PTSD symptoms also has a substance abuse problem, they are said to have dual disorders. The most effective therapies will treat both problems simultaneously since one disorder feeds the other.

In their book *Treating Addicted Survivors of Trauma*, authors Katie Evans and J. Michael Sullivan note:

> We and other writers in the area of "dual diagnosis" have consistently argued for an integrated treatment approach for clients suffering from substance abuse disorders and co-existing psychiatric disorders. Not only does the treatment need to address both illnesses simultaneously, but it must weave the treatment together in order to address the intertwined reality of these two fused conditions.

Urge your loved one to get help for both disorders if they are struggling with post-traumatic symptoms and chemical dependency, but regardless of their actions, *take care of yourself.* And if your loved one tries to use you as an excuse for their addictive behavior (you're always nagging; I've got PTSD and now you're adding to the pressure), remind yourself that—as was the case with the initial trauma—you did not cause, nor can you control, your loved one's addiction. If your life and household are being turned upside down by your loved one's dual problems, consider calling your therapist or attending a Twelve Step support group such as Al-Anon, Alateen, or Adult Children of Alcoholics (ACA). Such meetings are plentiful and are designed to offer guidance and support for spouses, parents, lovers, friends, and children (both young and older) of alcoholics. Similar groups like Nar-Anon are available for those whose loved ones are addicted to drugs (although families and friends of addicts can also attend Al-Anon).

A member of Al-Anon Family Groups put it this way in the book *In All Our Affairs: Making Crises Work for You:*

> Al-Anon does not promise to save marriages, only sanity! If you do want the marriage, they told me, then accept the fact that you will not get healthy behavior from a sick person or logical statements from an illogical person. This includes me too.
>
> With the help of the Al-Anon program, I am living one day at a time. I am also married one day at a time. This simplifies my life.

Even without the presence of dual disorders, a mutual-support group might help you cope with the day-to-day stress that comes with caring for a loved one who has post-traumatic symptoms. Since so many of the issues relating to trauma parallel the issues that relate to addiction (such as powerlessness, distorted thinking, out-of-control behavior), some people get help by using the Twelve Steps to admit their powerlessness over trauma and sort out how they can take care of themselves in the midst of trauma's fallout.

Detaching with Love

While survivors cannot help the fact that trauma has affected them, they are responsible for how they deal with those effects. You can learn to take responsibility for yourself even when your traumatized loved one is not acting responsibly and not getting help for their dual disorders. This self-care action is often called "detachment with love." A core recovery principle that has more general applications is that addicts and alcoholics cannot learn from their mistakes if they are overprotected. Overprotection might mean calling in sick for a spouse or friend who is high or hung over, or making up excuses for a loved one's embarrassing behavior (he's been under a lot of stress; she just needed to relax and let her hair down tonight). Such actions used to be called "enabling," because they enabled alcoholics or drug addicts to continue drinking and using. Today, the less-blaming term "adapting" is used to describe how we adjust our actions to cover up or excuse another's addictive behavior.

> *I thought I was doing pretty well coping with my wife's PTSD. I read all I could find about it and tried to be understanding and supportive when she had nightmares or rage attacks. I was a little worried about her mixing antidepressants with alcohol, but she always had a good excuse. She'd tell me it helped her sleep or it curbed her anxiety. Then I found out she was sneaking booze and smoking pot. I got a little crazy, doing things like spying on her or going through the trash for empties. I confronted her, and she felt bad and said she'd cut down. I felt like a policeman. When she got drunk at a party, I just blew. I love her, but I was so tired of planning my life around her ups and downs. Then a friend in Al-Anon suggested I go to a meeting with him. It's been a year now and things are so much better. Now my wife goes to AA and PTSD therapy, so we'll see. But whatever happens, I know I'll be okay.*

Detaching with love is one more way to establish healthy boundaries. It does not mean scaring the alcoholic or addict by threatening to leave if they don't get help. In fact, detachment with love is more about us than our traumatized and addicted loved one. It is about letting go of our attempts to control and instead sending a message with no ulterior motives: "I care about you enough to let you take responsibility for your own life, just as I take responsibility for mine."

....

QUESTIONS TO ASK YOURSELF ABOUT YOUR LOVED ONE'S ADDICTIVE BEHAVIOR

To help you determine if and how your loved one's addictive behavior is affecting your life, ask yourself these questions, adapted from information found on the Al-Anon Web site:

- Do you worry about how much someone else drinks or uses drugs or other aspects of their addictive behavior?
- Do you have money problems because of someone else's addictive behavior?
- Do you tell lies to cover up for someone else's addictive behavior?
- Do you feel that if the person cared about you, they would stop drinking or taking drugs or change their addictive behavior to please you?
- Do you blame the person's behavior on their companions?
- Are plans frequently upset or cancelled or meals delayed because of the person's addictive behavior?
- Do you make threats, such as "If you don't stop drinking or taking drugs, I'll leave you"?
- Do you secretly try to smell the drinker's breath?
- Are you afraid to upset someone for fear it will set off a binge of alcohol or other drug use or cause a relapse of addictive behavior?
- Have you been hurt or embarrassed by a person's under-the-influence or addictive behavior?
- Are holidays and gatherings spoiled because of your loved one's drinking or drug use, or addictive behavior?
- Have you considered calling the police for help in fear of abuse?
- Do you search for hidden alcohol or other drugs?
- Do you ever ride in a car with a driver who has been drinking or is under the influence of drugs?
- Have you refused social invitations out of fear or anxiety?
- Do you feel like a failure because you can't control your loved one's alcohol or other drug use or addictive behavior?
- Do you ever threaten to hurt yourself to scare the drinker or drug user?
- Do you feel angry, confused, or depressed most of the time?

- Do you feel there is no one who understands your problems?

  If you answered yes to any of these questions, a group such as Al-Anon (www.al-anon.alateen.org) or Nar-Anon (www.nar-anon.org) might be of interest and help. Twelve Step meetings are free and confidential.

....

Living Sanely, One Day at a Time

Someone said that insanity is doing the same thing over and over again, expecting different results, and that sanity is what we get when we quit hoping for a better past. We cannot change the fact that trauma affected our loved one and infected our life. But we can stop our unhealthy patterns of trying to control how our loved one deals (or doesn't deal) with the effects of the trauma and we can interrupt our own cycle of compulsive or codependent behavior. We can get sane. We can recover.

The word *addict* comes from the Latin word for *surrender*. At the height of addictive behavior, people surrender their will to a drug or a behavior or a person. Recovery is a new kind of surrender: surrender to the acceptance of help. Help from a therapist. Help from a Higher Power. Help from your healthy self. Help from a supportive community that welcomes your confusion and listens to your stories.

Al-Anon taught me I could think about emotional behavior as clearly as I could think about my son's PTSD or his drinking and cocaine habits. It taught me that codependent behavior is as real as a bottle of liquor or a coke spoon.

Recovery is a lifelong process that improves all aspects of ourselves: body, mind, and spirit. People in recovery don't say they are "recovered," but recovering, because they accept that life is tentative. Something can trigger our own relapse of compulsive behavior just as something can trigger our loved one's trauma symptoms. "Stuff" happens when you're least expecting it, but joy happens too. Recovery opens us to more fully appreciate the moments of grace and joy and strengthens us for the difficult times.

I am a Minnesotan, used to bundling up in the winter with hat and scarf, warm gloves, heavy coat, thick socks, and boots. Each spring I look forward to once again lightening that heavy load. This is how I view recovery. In recovery, we learn to let go of the attitudes and behaviors that weighed us down. We give up our need to control. We expose our distorted thinking. We release resentment and begin to understand how it grows from unresolved anger. We learn how toxic emotions—no matter how justified we might feel about having them—hurt us more than others. As Buddha said, "Holding on to anger is like grasping a hot coal with the intent of throwing it at someone else; you are the one who gets burned."

When we rid ourselves of negative behaviors and thoughts, we make more room for unconditional love and compassion—for others *and* for ourselves. Healthy relationships are hard work in the best of circumstances; tougher when the person we care about is suffering from the effects of trauma; and potentially disastrous when one or both are also engaged in an addictive or compulsive behavior.

Ultimately, recovery is about choice. Each day we can decide to blame trauma or our loved one for our actions and feelings or we can take responsibility for our own life and growth. What do you choose?

· ·

REFLECT ON YOUR JOURNEY OF RECOVERY

Read this excerpt and think about your own journey of recovery. Where and who are you now? Where do you need or want to go?

If we've been on a real journey—and we have—where are the postcards, the souvenirs, the tan lines? We are accustomed to having labels and anecdotes to dispense whenever someone asks who we are, what we do, what we have been up to lately. In the period of return, we have no handy labels. We have lost the ability to speak coherently about experience because we have traveled off the edge of any expectation we had, upon setting out, for what the journey would mean, would do, or where it would land us. . . .

This is a normal part of the journey. The old self-concept has broken down, and a new one is taking its place, which is harder to discuss and share with the world. You are coming into your soul. And that is exactly what is required because your life is changed and only your soul can adequately respond to the capabilities the journey has created in you.

—Christina Baldwin,
Life's Companion:
Journal Writing as a Spiritual Quest

If you want, go a little deeper by completing these phrases in writing:

- I used to be _____
- Now I am _____
- I want to be _____

....

CHAPTER 7

Trauma and Parenting

My Child, I Dream

She watches me sleep.
I know this, and I know
she approaches me with the heart
of a bird, that flutters more than it beats.
And I know this is because
she is afraid (must be afraid)
of my sleep.

I know this because she is there
with me sometimes,
staggering through the mud and confusion.
There is no safe place,
no way to escape the smell
of rotten canvas and death.
Or the quiet in my left ear.

With her I am NEVER angry. Because
with the heart of a bird,
she is afraid of my sleep.

—Jessica Orange

JESSICA WROTE "MY CHILD, I DREAM" as a bookend to "Waking Him"—the poem that introduced chapter 1. In the first poem, she describes how she learned early on not to startle her dad awake; how she knew to "begin the waking slowly" in order to bring Michael back into the present moment—into the safe world of "fenced in yards and refrigerator art." She wrote the above poem from Michael's perspective, imagining how fiercely he fought to protect her from his memories and PTSD reactions. Although she was a teenager when she wrote these poems, I think they poignantly reveal how keenly little children observe what's happening in a household affected by trauma and how they try to adjust their behavior accordingly.

Jessica was a toddler when Michael and I got married, and we naively assumed that she was too little to know what was going on if he dreamt or we talked about Vietnam. When she did become more aware, we (also naively) thought if we didn't discuss things in front of her, she would be unaffected. Beware the assumptive world.

In writing this book, I spoke with a clinical social worker from New York who worked with teachers and children in schools close to the World Trade Center site after the 9/11 terrorist attack and who also works with orphaned children in Rwanda. He explained that the effects of trauma can be transmitted to children unconsciously through the verbal and the unspoken messages we send—usually unintentionally.

I worked with a woman who was diagnosed with breast cancer when her children were very young. Her two-year-old started becoming very symptomatic—crying a lot, having temper tantrums, and acting out in other ways. As I worked more with the mother, it became clear that she had suffered other traumas during her life, and her little girl's behaviors were linked to the mother's post-traumatic symptoms and the trauma of the cancer diagnosis. Without consciously knowing it or being able to articulate it, the little girl had absorbed some of the mother's trauma.

Unknown thought is a term that was first coined in 1987 by psychoanalyst Christopher Bollas to describe what we know but for a number of reasons may not be able to consciously think yet, or that which we intuitively sense but cannot yet articulate. In other words—as was the case with the two-year-old in the above example—we may know something but don't yet know that we know it. Often, our bodies or behaviors give clues about this hidden knowledge.

Whatever the term for this mysterious process, it is important to realize that children—no matter their age or level of development—are sponges. As Jessica's poems show, she grasped her dad's anguish and instinctively knew how to react, even though she couldn't put words to these instincts or understand them until she was much older. I can still remember how Michael and I wept when we first read these poems. Our hearts ached when we realized how widespread are the shock wave effects of trauma, yet we were also relieved that, despite this reality, our daughter was secure in the knowledge that Michael loved her unconditionally and that he would do all he could to protect her.

Children and Trauma

In my mind, I can still see the picture of the rescue worker carrying the injured child out of the Murrah Building after the Oklahoma City bombing. I still remember the heartbreaking news stories about how kids in schools near the twin towers in New York drew pictures after 9/11—turning the bodies they had seen falling from the towers' windows into birds and angels in their drawings. And I, like so many other Minnesotans, held my breath as a school bus carrying children on a summer field trip rested precariously on the edge of the I-35 bridge in Minneapolis when it collapsed into the Mississippi River on August 1, 2007, and breathed a sigh of relief when we saw the kids being carried to safety. When trauma strikes—whether on a large scale or in one home in one city—we worry about the littlest witnesses and how they will handle all they've seen or experienced.

On its Web site (www.nctsn.org), the National Child Traumatic

Stress Network estimates that one out of four children in this country experiences a serious traumatic event by age sixteen, and many
of them suffer multiple traumas. While most children adapt and
recover from these experiences, some develop child traumatic stress
(CTS)—a psychological reaction like PTSD with symptoms that
linger and affect their daily lives long after the traumatic event has
ended. We now know—and as many of the people who shared their
stories for this book related—that a person who experiences a childhood trauma is more vulnerable as an adult to the effects of subse-
quent traumas.

> *When I finally got help for PTSD from the war, my therapist—
> after a few sessions—urged me to talk about my childhood
> trauma. He said I was having difficulty healing from my psychic
> wounds from war because I had not healed from that earlier
> trauma. He said it was as if Vietnam had refractured a knee that
> had not healed properly from an earlier injury and that in the
> safety of his therapist's office we would tend to both traumas and
> carefully see it through to a complete healing. "You may still walk
> with a slight limp," he told me, "but you'll walk fully upright."*

Experts have also learned more about how a loved one's trauma
can affect a child. For example, researchers who study combat-related
PTSD have found that children of parents with PTSD typically respond to their parents' trauma symptoms in three ways:

1. The child experiences secondary traumatization and
   comes to experience many of the symptoms the parent
   with PTSD exhibits;
2. The child assumes the role of the "rescuer," taking on
   parental roles and responsibilities to compensate for the
   parent's difficulties; and
3. The child becomes emotionally uninvolved because he or
   she is getting little emotional support, which results in

problems at school, depression and anxiety, and relational problems later in life. Chaos at home can make it difficult for children to establish positive attachments to parents, which, in turn, can make it harder for children to create healthy relationships.

I am aware that trauma in childhood increases vulnerability to further trauma—including accidents and illnesses. Witnessing the abuse in my home made me shy and socially inept, which contributed to my being identified in junior high as the target for mean girls who did things like jump me, take off my clothes, and mock my less-developed body. I was also injured in a car accident in college and had a life-threatening illness. I developed an eating disorder, depression, and was diagnosed with PTSD in my thirties.

Studies of Vietnam veterans with PTSD have shown there is significantly more violence in these families than in families of veterans without PTSD, including increased violent behavior among the children of these veterans. Research has also revealed that children of parents with PTSD are at a higher risk for behavioral, academic, and interpersonal problems.

Things are even more difficult for children in homes where a parent's trauma symptoms marry their addictive behaviors. John Bradshaw puts it this way in his book *Bradshaw On: The Family—A New Way of Creating Solid Self-Esteem:*

The alcoholic family is a compulsive family. Everyone in the system is affected by the distress caused by the anxiety over the alcoholic's drinking. Someone compared living in an alcoholic family to living in a concentration camp. And like survivors of a concentration camp ACAs [adult children of alcoholics] carry what has been compared to post-traumatic stress symptoms. In fact, if one takes a list of the disorders experienced by war veterans or any other severe trauma victims, one will find that a large number of the post-trauma symptoms match a large number of the ACoA characteristics. Children who live in alcoholic families, if untreated as children, carry these characteristics of post-trauma stress into later life.

We know that too often, children of substance abusers learn the "four Ds" early on: Don't talk about what is really going on. Don't trust anyone but yourself. Don't feel or have needs because there is no one available to validate or respond to you. Deny there is a problem. When you add trauma symptoms and other addictive behaviors to the mix, these messages get even more pronounced. Notice how the four Ds mirror the post-traumatic symptoms of avoidance and numbing.

> *My dad did three tours in Vietnam. He was very isolated when he came home and was drunk much of the time. He'd get angry at anything and he'd go weeks without talking to anyone. He never showed his feelings toward Mom or my twin brother or myself. He could never say "I love you" because I think he thought he might lose us like he lost his buddies in the war. I had a lot of anger issues myself—I think I thought it was okay to get mad because that's what my dad did. I have a hard time showing my emotions too. Now I'm a combat vet home from Iraq. I got diagnosed with PTSD a few months ago and I'm also in treatment for alcoholism. But I'm getting better one day at a time.*

Members in a household affected by trauma often lose sight of what is "normal." In an effort to not upset the traumatized parent or to not further disrupt an already chaotic household, children might try to be perfect. Or they might copy some of the same angry or aggressive behaviors and attitudes of their traumatized parent. Older children may try to escape family chaos by abusing illegal drugs or alcohol or practicing some other addictive behavior. Younger children might become insecure and clingy. Some may be so worried about their parent or upset about the trauma that they have difficulty concentrating at school, or they begin to develop post-traumatic symptoms of their own. They might have nightmares, suffer from anxiety or depression, become overly fearful, or experience other physical symptoms.

If one or both parents have shut down emotionally in the aftermath of a trauma, children hungry for affection may seek approval or affirmation elsewhere—often from the wrong people. Children of parents affected by trauma may also have trouble identifying or expressing their own feelings because feelings aren't discussed or shown at home. It's crucial for a child to hear parental sentiments like "I'm sorry," or "I love you," but these might be absent or seem meaningless if they are delivered without emotion or behaviors consistent with such statements. A child may further withdraw if a parent's initial trauma was so great that they treat the child's day-to-day problems as trivial by comparison.

According to the National Center for PTSD, family members of trauma survivors might have surprisingly negative feelings about the traumatized family member because they are upset about the changes in their loved one.

> *My relationship with my kids is strained right now. On a recent vacation they joined forces to tell me to stop talking about the crash and quit dwelling on my husband's absence. After being soundly chewed out by them, I was even sadder and more upset. They think I should just get over it and go back to the way I was before. If their father was still here they would never talk to me like they have been lately.*

The economic insecurity so widespread in these financially unstable times is also having a stressful—even traumatic—effect on many children today. Researchers estimate that two million children might be affected by this country's foreclosure crisis. Jobless parents are often forced to relocate, and already worried children are made more anxious as they try to adjust to new schools and lifestyles.

> *I'm so concerned about the kids and the stress they are showing in these tough economic times. Just the one school district in Florida, where I teach, helped about 2,450 homeless students last year and they say that could double this year. That's nearly 5,000 students who don't know where they'll sleep or how they'll get to school. And that's just in one county and it's reflected across our state. One of my kindergarten students came in so tired one day that he actually fell asleep while sitting on the rug. When I asked him if he was okay, he told me he didn't get much sleep because he and his sister had to go with Mom to his grandma's house in the middle of the night. His dad got really mad and was hitting his mom. I followed up with the mother and she said her husband—who had never acted like that before—had lost his job and they might lose their house. His anxiety, depression, and sleeplessness were coming out as anger. How can learning and focusing on lessons be a priority for these kids when they are in situations like this?*

More than likely, your children are more aware of what's going on than you give them credit for, but they're still children—not short adults. It is difficult enough for us to understand the significance and widespread effects of our loved one's trauma; we can only imagine how confusing it must be for a child who worries why Mom or Dad is acting differently in the aftermath of trauma. More than ever, they—just like us—need all the love, reassurance, and support they can get.

Toward Positive Parenting
It's tough to parent under the best of circumstances, but even tougher for a parent who has the added challenge of caring for and supporting a loved one with post-traumatic symptoms. No doubt, there will be days when your loved one is unwilling or unable to help you with

your children and you might feel like a single parent. At such times, it is even more important to take good care of yourself.

> *My husband is in therapy for PTSD and he is improving, but he still has a short fuse and shuts down emotionally. My young son asked me why Daddy was mad all the time, and my teenage daughter thought she was doing something wrong and internalizing everything. We keep assuring them that we love them and got counseling for my daughter who began to act out a lot. But so many times I feel alone in all of this. I know that if I don't take care of myself, I won't be able to take care of my children, but it's hard to do that sometimes.*

When you are feeling overwhelmed by childcare and other responsibilities, reread the chapters on self-care. It is also helpful to educate yourself about the effects of trauma on children so you will be better prepared to identify problems, answer questions, and offer reassurances when the need arises. A good start is to download the free booklet offered by the National Institute of Mental Health (NIMH) titled *Helping Children and Adolescents Cope With Violence and Disasters: What Parents Can Do* (www.nimh.nih.gov/health/ publications/helping-children-and-adolescents-cope-with-violence-and-disasters-what-parents-can-do/index.shtml). While this information is directed toward helping young survivors of trauma, the guidance offered can easily be applied to children who may be suffering the trickle-down effects from a parent's trauma.

Breathe deeply, remember the oxygen mask metaphor, and ask for help when you need it. Asking for help with your children when you are physically exhausted and emotionally overwhelmed is a sign of strength and good judgment—*not* failure. A child can never be loved too much or by too many, so consider enlisting the help of a "big friend" or mentor when you think your child is in need of a little extra tender, loving care. Big friends are not substitutes for you or your loved one; they are responsive and responsible adults who can provide support, friendship, reinforcement, positive role modeling, and companionship. Research on adolescent development has indicated that a relationship with at least one caring adult, not necessarily a parent, is perhaps the single most important element in protecting young people who have multiple risks in their lives.

While I believe my trauma created some fantasies of being rescued, the best kind of help I received was not quite rescue, but rather attention to what I needed. I vividly remember the adults who gave me validation and encouragement. My second grade teacher was playful and told me she hoped she could see what I would become when I grew up. I felt supported by a cranky but caring high school band leader—himself a polio survivor. I even remember taking encouragement when the local butcher commented on my work in a theater production, telling me, "You were just the shits!"

Successful mentors build on the values and strengths you've worked so hard to instill in your child and work in harmony with you to offer safety and reassurance to a child who may be feeling the effects of your loved one's traumatic experience.

As a child, the deepest pain of my trauma was its invisibility—and all the ways I learned to keep it that way. I would love to have had the attention of a caring person who was clearly there for my own sake—not on their own agenda. I would like to have had someone reassure me that what was going on around me was crazy and it was hard—but that I was okay. I wish someone had told me that trauma will lie to you. It might tell you [that you] are to blame; that no one wants to hear about it; that you do not deserve help; that you can't be good to yourself until it is fixed; that if you do enough it will be better. I wish someone had told me that trauma can be a big, and most convincing liar.

Mentors might be your trusted friends or relatives or one of your child's teachers or a guidance counselor. If you do not have family or friends close by or available, you might consider a more structured relationship by contacting an organization like Big Brothers or Big Sisters (www.bbbsa.org), which has rigorous standards for their volunteers by requiring references and training to ensure the match will be appropriate and safe for your child. The National Mentoring Partnership (www.mentoring.org) can also direct you to local partnerships in your area.

> *Many years ago, our nephew stayed with us after a traumatic episode in his home. We didn't push him to talk, but let him know we were there if he wanted to. Mostly, we went on with our lives, including him in all our family activities and making sure there was structure to his days and that he felt safe and loved. We didn't really know what it meant to him because he was pretty young. He's an adult now and told me recently that he always thought of us and our home as sanctuary for him. I just cried and hugged him. It meant so much to hear that.*

Positive peer relationships are also important for children of traumatized parents. The clinical social worker I interviewed said he was amazed at how so many of the Rwandan orphans he worked with flourished as they relied upon and nurtured each other in the absence of parental attachments. He compared it to a blind person whose brain rewires to develop an extra or heightened sense of touch. While the children certainly missed and grieved their absent parents, they were able to provide comfort and safety to each other.

A goal in parenting (not just after a trauma but all the time) is to create a safe place for your children without smothering them or abandoning them. Practicing positive parenting builds your own self-esteem, helps your children build self-esteem, and builds resilience in you and your children. In his book *Lost Boys: Why Our Sons Turn Violent and How We Can Save Them*, James Garbarino defines resiliency as "the ability to bounce back from crisis and overcome stress and injury." He said that to be resilient, children need spiritual, psychological, and social anchors that connect them to positive values and relationships.

Spiritual anchors give deeper meaning to children's lives and help them sort through the tough questions like "Who am I?" Psychological anchors include authentic self-esteem, constructive coping strategies, intellectual ability, the capacity to actively respond to events rather than passively react to them, an ability to seek social support from outside the family, and having someone who is crazy about them. Social anchors are found in the social health of families, schools, and communities, and include adults who commit themselves unconditionally to meeting a child's developmental needs.

Children of a traumatized parent may feel particularly vulnerable when that parent exhibits post-traumatic symptoms. We can foster resiliency, but we should never expect it.

> *I'm not big on labels like "disorder" or "resilient," although they do provide an entryway for discussion and diagnosis. We just need to be careful they don't create an "otherness." I worked with a young man who recounted a horrific story of genocide where all five siblings and his parents were killed. Yes, he's bright and "resilient," but the pain is always there and his post-traumatic symptoms could still be triggered. It's not a dichotomy—we can be resilient and, at the same time, hold an overwhelming woundedness within us.*

When a parent has experienced a trauma, children need to be reassured that *they* are safe and loved and that Mommy or Daddy's behavior has nothing to do with them. Go slowly and take your cues from them. When it's appropriate or necessary, you can talk to your children about what's going on with your loved one in simple terms that they can understand. A child's anxiety may increase when a parent avoids discussions of the trauma or silences questions. Without understanding the reasons for their parent's symptoms, children may create their own ideas about the trauma, which can be even more horrifying than what actually occurred. Saying too much about the trauma can also be a problem, so avoid graphic details. How much you tell your child should be influenced by the child's age and maturity level.

It's also best to avoid television or other news accounts if the trauma is covered in the news. Studies done after 9/11 revealed that children all over the country were anxious and afraid because of the nonstop news coverage, and younger children thought there were many planes and many attacks because they kept seeing the same images over and over again.

If your loved one has nightmares or triggers, you can offer simple explanations so your children will not be unduly frightened when a reaction occurs. "Daddy gets a little jumpy from loud noises because of the loud noises he heard in the war, but he doesn't mean to scare you."

Try to be a respectful listener when your children want to talk about feelings, and not dismiss or discount what they tell you by telling them a feeling is silly or they should "just get over it." You may want to encourage them to write about their feelings or draw pictures—but don't force children to discuss how they're feeling about your loved one's trauma before they are ready. If you sense your child needs to talk about feelings but is unable to express them to you or your loved one, enlist the support of the school guidance counselor or a therapist who is familiar with the effects of trauma on a family.

Consider grief counseling if your family has experienced the death of a loved one and your child is having difficulty dealing with this loss.

Check with your child's school guidance counselor or your local social service agency if your family is suffering traumatic effects from the economic crisis. Many agencies provide school supplies and clothes, and can help with other needs. You can contact United Way in many states by simply calling 211 for help with and information on social services or visiting www.211.org to find out more about your local 211 service.

Also let your children's teacher know what is going on at home because it might be affecting their behavior at school.

> *If we teachers know there is a reason for what could be going on, we can be more sympathetic or handle it in a different way. Parents may be able to suggest ways that they've found to be successful in helping or reassuring the child. Sometimes when a parent has a problem, they can contact the guidance counselor or school psychologist without the teacher being informed. It's often not necessary to go into detail about the trauma, just a simple, "We've had a lot going on at home, so Susie might be tired or emotional" could be enough for the person who deals with the child on a daily basis. You'd be surprised how many times people assume the teacher has been informed, when they actually have no idea what's going on at home. The teacher only knows that the child is having problems in the classroom.*

Allow your children to be sad and comfort them when they cry. Try to be as patient as you can if a child reverts to younger behaviors. Children might need to sleep with a light on or require a little extra attention if they are having difficulty sleeping.

Try to keep up normal routines such as bedtime stories, and if you can't keep up the normal routines, consider establishing new ones that provide comfort and reassurance. Help children feel in control by letting them choose meals, pick out clothes, or make some decisions for themselves when appropriate. Finally, make sure your children know that it is a parent's job to solve the problems surrounding your loved one's post-traumatic reactions—not theirs. Reassure them—as you reassured yourself—that they didn't cause the trauma and they cannot, nor are they expected to, cure it.

EDUCATE YOURSELF ABOUT TRAUMA'S EFFECTS ON CHILDREN

As the NIMH stresses in its booklet *Helping Children and Adolescents Cope With Violence and Disasters: What Parents Can Do,* children's reactions to traumatic events vary widely, depending on their age, level of maturity, severity of trauma, or cultural practices.

- Very young children (under age five) are strongly influenced by a parent's reaction to a traumatic event, and could return to behaviors such as thumb sucking or bed-wetting. They might also cry a lot and become clingy.
- Children between ages six and eleven might become quiet and isolate themselves, have nightmares or sleep problems, become angry or disruptive, refuse to go to school or do poorly in school, complain of unfounded physical problems, be depressed or emotionally numb, or feel guilty.
- Adolescents ages twelve to seventeen might also turn to alcohol or other drugs or tobacco use, or experience suicidal thoughts or thoughts of revenge.

Some children may need help from a mental health professional who knows how to help kids who are dealing with a parent's PTSD. Review the guidelines for choosing a therapist on pages 86–87 if you think your child is in need of counseling.

If your loved one is in the military, Operation Military Kids (OMK) might be of help. This is the U.S. Army's collaborative effort with America's communities to support the children and youth impacted by deployment. Since its Web site (www .operationmilitarykids.org) was launched in 2005, OMK reports the organization touched 88,000 military youth and provided information to 21,009 communities throughout the United States.

Teachable Moments

It is natural to want to shield our children from the difficult lessons of life—to pluck the thorns from the roses so they won't get pricked by painful experiences. No matter how vigorously we try, we can't protect them from every life trial, but we can model for them how to meet challenges and, most importantly, how to care for oneself and how to ask for help.

We can also take advantage of teachable moments—those times when children are most ready to learn. These moments can be big or small, any time something happens to children that triggers confusion, curiosity, or conflict. For example, such a moment might occur when your child appears worried or confused after seeing your loved one jump, tremble, cry, and leave the room abruptly at the sight of a car crash on television. By speaking honestly to your children, using "I" statements that address *your* feelings and beliefs rather than telling your children how *they* should feel or what they should believe, you can use the opportunity to give valuable information to your children about the effects of trauma.

You might say something like, "I get a little worried about Mommy when she seems scared by what she sees on television or when she jumps at loud noises, but she still gets upset because of her car accident. She isn't angry with us for watching TV or for anything we said or did." You could also follow this with an open-ended question, like, "How did you feel when Mommy got upset?"

Teachable moments provide good opportunities to practice communication techniques and listening skills we've already discussed. They are chances to connect with our children on a deeper level; to offer reassurances and let them know how we feel and to find out more about how they are feeling about the trauma. You can learn to identify teachable moments by paying attention to your children's faces and body language. If your child's face is scrunched up in confusion or bright with obvious curiosity, or if it's obvious from their body language or facial expression that they are having some sort of inner conflict, the time is ripe for a teachable moment. If, however, you are met with blank faces and faraway stares, the lesson would likely be lost on them.

Each attempt at connection and display of compassion, each time we listen respectfully, and each time we take advantage of a teachable moment, we add to the bouquet we present to our children—the skills and tools and lessons we give them that will help them grow strong and healthy.

Positive parenting, like all other aspects of this journey from trauma to healing, is about progress not perfection. Progress, not perfection. Progress, not perfection. Say it with feeling, capture the rhythm of the phrase. It chugs along like the little engine in the story you used to read—or still read—to your children. The goal for parents is to move forward, one day, one experience, and, yes, even one mistake, at a time. You will not be a perfect parent. Your children will not be perfect children. But you can be a loving parent and a healthy human being.

····························

CHAPTER 8

Rebuilding Your Life

For nothing is fixed, forever and forever and forever, it is not fixed; the earth is always shifting, the light is always changing, the sea does not cease to grind down rock. Generations do not cease to be born, and we are responsible to them because we are the only witnesses they have. The sea rises, the light fails, lovers cling to each other, and children cling to us. The moment we cease to hold each other, the moment we break faith with one another, the sea engulfs us and the light goes out.

—JAMES BALDWIN,
"Nothing Personal"

I REMEMBER A DISCUSSION AFTER 9/11 about the word *closure*, and how ambiguous the term seemed to me. Some mental health professionals were criticized for urging the survivors—and the whole country, for that matter—to achieve closure before people had a chance to process the enormity of what had transpired that fateful September day. A traumatic event may be long over, but that doesn't mean we're finished with its effects.

I've discovered there is no blueprint for healing. I think closure is a meaningless term. I can't—I won't—forget what happened and all those we lost in the Oklahoma City bombing. It's been important for me to work on the memorial and to revisit it each anniversary. It's part of my healing. I did an interview with a lady who is writing a book about the death penalty and she wondered if I felt closure after Timothy McVeigh [one of the bombers] was executed. I told her that I—and many others I know close to trauma—really have a problem with that term. Media, experts, our friends, and even some family members want to put time frames on grief. There is no such thing as closure, in my opinion, when it comes to trauma and loss. What matters is how you deal with that loss or grief.

It's been forty years since Michael served in Vietnam, and I know its impact will always be with us. Granted, the effects of that war do not have us in the stranglehold they once did, but Michael's experiences are a part of who we are—individually and as partners. Each time we meet one more traumatized person, each time we see images of war, we are poignantly brought back to our own journeys of trauma and healing, which helps us build a bridge of compassion and more genuinely support others who suffer deep loss. As a wise person said, "Trauma may always be with you, but you can carry it differently."

Trauma continues to inform our lives, and we can grow from its lessons.

I may reject the concept of closure when it comes to trauma, but I can embrace the importance of *acknowledgment*. Someone said that experience is what you get when you don't get what you want. No one wants trauma. I will never be thankful that trauma injured our lives, yet I acknowledge that it did and that I am powerless to undo what has already happened. "You can't change the wind, but you can adjust the sails" is a saying heard often in recovery groups. Acknowledging the depth of change in my life that resulted from Michael's trauma is a way to adjust my sails to accommodate the presence of trauma, and chart a new course. This frees me to go on living—and loving—my life, though I will never *get over* what we've experienced. I'm not expecting closure.

The opposite of acknowledgment is denial—that seductive

"Pollyanna" mindset where we try to convince ourselves and others that everything is just fine, even though our lives say otherwise. Beware of slipping from acknowledgment to denial by putting a time frame on your own or your loved one's healing. We might impede recovery or be less able to handle triggers if we tell ourselves we are or *should* be over the effects of trauma.

I saw a friend recently who is still abusing alcohol and unable to work because of PTSD. When I asked her how she was, she quickly responded, "I'm great. I'm done with all of that." When we deny the ongoing reality of trauma, we discount or invalidate our own or another's experience. Acknowledgment is not resignation or something we do once and then are done. As with most things human, dealing with trauma is a fluid practice. It involves both the process of acknowledgment gained through a deep exploration of the trauma experience and its shock wave effects, and the practice of stitching it into the larger tapestry of our lives. With time and continued effort, trauma's effects can become more manageable, and acknowledgment can become the foundation for growth and action. For me, this means that while trauma does not define me, it *is* a part of me.

> *We're living in a different state now and making new friends. I don't need to be fawned over and I don't want sympathy, but a part of me does need people to know that my husband is a trauma survivor and realize this was a life-changing event. It's a part of who I am now.*

Healing from trauma's effects is a process of reclaiming and mending—and ultimately rebuilding—the lives of trauma survivors and those who love them. *Reclaim* means to retrieve something that has been taken away or temporarily given to someone or something else, and *mend* means to improve something or make it more tolerable.

> *I will always cherish a comment made by a friend who watched me walk with what felt like excruciating slowness when I was*

released from the hospital and was still physically very weak. It is lovely, she said, to see you carry yourself with such reverence. This is perhaps one of the best therapeutic "reframings" I have experienced. I believe this reframing is a powerful and evolving process in the healing of trauma.

Trauma takes things from us—among them, time, security, trust, certainty, and a sense of self—and leaves in its place doubt, fear, loss, and confusion, and new responsibilities. But we're still standing—even if we might feel a little wobbly. As you educate yourself about trauma and its effects, mourn your losses, and learn new skills, I hope you're getting braver, more confident, and more comfortable in your own skin.

I've been lucky to have the guidance of a great therapist. He is so caring, and he's helped me be more caring toward myself. I remember what he said after the first time I told him a really painful story. He said, "We need to go back and unpack your story with great compassion. We need to slow it down and focus on the emotional connections. When you had that shattering experience as a young girl, your whole world shattered." Over time, I learned to slow down the video version of my stories and see how they were interconnected with my past and much more complex than I realized.

Again, the process is the same for the loved ones of a trauma survivor. We are the authors of our own story. With the appropriate help and guidance, we can come to a fuller understanding of our loved one's trauma and its impact on us. After much slow and thoughtful work, we can deconstruct our story and try to integrate it into the larger story of our lives.

Taking a Risk

When we bring compassion to our own story, we can change our perspective of it, and we can also change the way we view and live in the present. Healing grows as we learn to respect and live with the pain of the past and simultaneously embrace and celebrate the joy life still holds. It is a slow and deliberate process. We need to come out of our caves slowly, squint at the light, and risk opening ourselves to others, to new experiences, and to moving forward. By itself, the word *risk* might sound scary or negative. But if you take the word letter by letter and make an acronym out of it, RISK becomes a positive call to action:

R—Relax and enjoy the adventure
I—Imagine the possibilities
S—Surrender the need to control
K—Know that you are not alone

When I had been in therapy for a while and was feeling a little more confident and less consumed with worry about Michael, I rented a cello. I was in my fifties and hadn't taken a music lesson since the fourth grade, when I played viola one summer. I found a teacher and once a week I screeched out songs like *Twinkle, Twinkle Little Star* and *Go Tell Aunt Rhody*. I was terrible at it, but I was gleeful—doing something I had always wanted to do. I even got brave enough to play my simple tunes for friends. I was, at last, making room for new experiences. I was finally starting to reconnect to myself and to the world around me.

Risk-taking need not be something huge like bungee jumping. It can be as small as contacting a friend from whom you distanced yourself when you and your loved one needed time and space to do the hard work you have been doing. Think about what little action you want to take today, then take a deep breath and go for it. Take a risk.

Practicing Self-Gratitude
In the early stages of dealing with the effects of a loved one's post-traumatic symptoms, the world and its stressors are very much with us. Our focus is necessarily external—directed toward the trauma

and our loved ones. When we begin to move toward self-care, we turn inward. This internal work is just as necessary, and it is ongoing. As we grow stronger in our recovery and healthier about balance and boundaries, there comes a time when we feel ready to reenter the world. We take time off from trauma and attempt to find a healthy balance between internal and external.

It's easy to lose sight of who we were (and who we were becoming) before trauma invaded our lives and we stepped forward to support our loved ones on their trauma journey. I remember being so enmeshed in Michael's life and problems after his PTSD diagnosis that if someone asked how *I* was, I would reply by telling them how *he* was doing or how we were handling his PTSD. The truth is, I didn't know how I was—or, for that matter, *who* I was outside of trauma.

Looking back, I think I had difficulty defining or describing myself because profound experiences like trauma require us to use resources we didn't know we had. I was in the midst of an evolutionary process—*me* at the core, but becoming a changed me.

Who are you now? The fact that you are reading this book means you are a curious and compassionate person. I urge you to embrace yourself with that same tenderness and, when the time is right and you are feeling ready, allow yourself to consider how you've changed. Set aside your humility for a moment and give yourself credit for all the things you've done that you didn't think you could do or had never done before.

My brother has blown me away. He's always been such a chauvinist—expecting his wife to handle all household responsibilities, even after they retired. One of his favorite sayings was, "Things are equal around here. She cooks the food and I eat it." But since the accident and her permanent disability, he's really stepped up to the plate. He schedules and gets her to appointments and keeps all her meds straight. He keeps their house and finances in order. And he doesn't seem resentful—just grateful she's alive. Who says you can't teach an old dog new tricks?

This is not to suggest that living with a loved one's trauma makes us eligible for sainthood. I still have crabby days when I feel put out or put upon by something related to Michael's PTSD or the war, and my behavior becomes less than noble. It's easy at those times to blow up at Michael and slip into "you" language, blaming him or Vietnam for my misery. When those moments eventually pass, though, I am getting better at taking responsibility for my reactions and figuring out why I had those intense feelings.

Sometimes I even discover that my crabbiness had less to do with trauma and more to do with some other stressor or the simple fact that I had too much coffee and not enough sleep. And if my feelings *are* trauma-related, I'll suggest we talk about that so we can work through it together. In the past, I could too easily slip from a bad mood to anger, depression, or self-loathing when such moments arose. Now I try to remind myself—once again—that this journey is about progress, not perfection; it's about communication, not blame or stuffing your emotions.

I still think trauma is too high a price to pay for any lessons it teaches or strengths we muster because of it. I do get great satisfaction, however, from knowing we can—and do—grow in spite of its presence. Growing stronger in the midst of trauma is like giving it the finger: saying "I hate you and what you've done to my family, but I'm determined you won't get the better of me." There's power in that.

....

APPRECIATE YOURSELF

Chapter 2 was about grief and mourning what you've lost as a result of your loved one's trauma—especially your sense of self. Although you may not yet realize it, you've gained things on this journey too. You've probably honed skills you didn't know you had, enlarged or adopted new qualities, developed new insights and outlooks, and increased your knowledge and understanding about trauma and its effects on an entire family system.

Think about the challenges you've faced related to your loved one's trauma and the ways in which you met those challenges. What strengths or skills do you have today that you didn't have before? Are you more organized or a better researcher? Can you assert yourself better with people in authority because you've had to be an advocate for your loved one or yourself? Are you a more compassionate and attentive listener? Can you express your wants or needs or feelings more clearly? Are you more determined to resolve conflicts through discussion instead of blaming or stuffing your feelings? Are you more patient, honest, or loving? Are you easier on yourself?

In recovery groups, you are urged to practice an "attitude of gratitude." Practice an attitude of self-gratitude today for all you've become and all you've accomplished.

....

Reconnecting with Others

One of Michael's most important tasks in therapy was to *do* less and *be* more; to unhook from compulsive busyness and slow down so he could—at last—face and understand the role trauma played in his life and in our relationship. His life got simpler and slower as he did the hard work his intense therapy required, and my life slowed down and simplified too. It's been good for both of us. We grew closer and emerged from the experience better able to make healthy choices about how we want to spend our time together and apart, and how much of that time we want to devote to our family (of relatives and of friends). This sifting and shifting of priorities while recovering from trauma is not unique to us.

So many of the remarkable people I've encountered in writing this book describe how their priorities have changed in the aftermath of trauma. As trauma survivors and those who love them adjust their already busy lives to deal with the effects of trauma, they get better at sorting out what and who are most important.

My son was killed in a fight at an off-campus party six years ago, and I'm still in grief therapy. Losing a child brought life's precariousness and briefness more into my awareness. I believe the trauma affected my desire to work full time—I realized there is so much more in life besides work. The tragedy hit my dad hard, too, but brought us closer. I'm also closer with my two adult children and my ex-wife now.

Trauma can change the lens through which we view relationships—especially when it comes to families. As we get healthier, we can better define what a healthy family looks like. This redefinition frees us to deepen or improve our relationship with our family of origin if that is what we choose, or invest more energy in our family of friends if that is the less toxic and more nurturing choice.

Learning about the roots and effects of trauma after my wife's memories started to surface and she was diagnosed with PTSD has helped us see just how unhealthy her family environment is. We've decided it's not good for us—and it's especially bad for our children—to be around them very much. There are some relatives we intentionally avoid altogether now. We still put in an occasional appearance at big family gatherings and we're all quite civil, but we consider our circle of close friends our truer family.

Our definition of family changes as our circumstances change. Parents die, children grow up and relocate. Part of rebuilding our life after trauma is deciding who we want to embrace as family. We can reclaim the word *family* and shape it to fit our life, our relationships, and our reality. Today, I consider my family to be those friends and relatives who share a bond of mutual support and unconditional love—a bond that transcends biology or marriage. They provide a safe place in which to feel and express a range of diverse thoughts and feelings. They are a team that values all members who care for each other in good times *and* bad.

I was single with no girlfriend when I was randomly shot. My parents lived 1,300 miles away, but I had really close friends. One arranged meals to be delivered to me for four straight weeks since I couldn't stand long enough to cook. My best friend came over and hung out with me numerous times. He just let me vent. He had never been through anything like this, so it was hard on him. But he hung with me. Since he knew me from before, he also pushed me to break the bad cycles and get back to my good life. He helped me progress when I felt all I'd been doing was going backwards.

Who do you include in your family? Who nurtures you, and who do you nurture? Who keeps you going forward as you continue to heal from the shock wave effects from trauma?

Human beings are social creatures who thrive on interaction. Caring for your loved one, your family, your job, yourself, and your many other responsibilities takes enormous time and energy, and it is understandable if you've been a little removed from the social scene. I know I was. Eventually, I felt like I wanted and needed to reconnect with friends.

Worthwhile friendships also take time, but it is time well spent. In fact, studies have shown that older people with a large circle of friends live longer than those with fewer friends. The most successful friendships tend to be the most adaptable and balanced ones. My friends are islands of sanctuary and distraction. I can talk about trauma when I need to, and, at other times, we can just hang out. And when they have something serious they want to discuss, I can now be more present with them.

In large part, our close friends and family members got Michael and me through the darkest hours when we felt our lives were spinning out of control. They were—and they continue to be—our lifelines. We discovered for ourselves what Judith Lewis Herman described in her book *Trauma and Recovery:*

> Those who have survived [trauma] learn that their sense
> of self, of worth, of humanity, depends upon a feeling of

connection to others. The solidarity of a group provides the strongest protection against terror and despair, and the strongest antidote to traumatic experience. . . .

Repeatedly in the testimony of survivors there comes a moment when a sense of connection is restored by another person's unaffected display of generosity. Something in herself that the victim believes to be irretrievably destroyed—faith, decency, courage—is reawakened by an example of common altruism. Mirrored in the actions of others, the survivor recognizes and reclaims a lost part of herself.

When a long-time and well-loved friend was diagnosed with a malignant brain tumor, her large community of friends and neighbors reeled from, then rallied around, the trauma. The guy she had "gone steady" with for forty-two years proposed, and in just weeks we put on a wedding for 250 people. Her exercise group became the decorating committee. Area musicians in the small town in which they lived gathered to play at the ceremony and reception. Local farmers cooked and catered, and city friends made a gorgeous cake. Bouquets were assembled, tables were decorated, lights were strung, and the wedding tent looked magical. White-haired friends from our hippie days became groomsmen, and with little notice, her bridesmaids combed their closets for dresses. Tears flowed, but the bride beamed, as we sang the couple down the aisle to her requested song, Zip-a-Dee-Doo-Dah.

This celebration felt like a barn raising—we were building a shelter for our friend big enough to hold the pain and fear of trauma alongside the joy and love of community. This experience was also a gift to Michael and me. It felt so good to be strong enough in our own journey of healing that we could reach out to help other loved ones who struggled with their own trauma. Trauma no longer dominates my life, thoughts, or discussions with friends, but I think that dealing with trauma has helped me be a better friend.

Navigating Trauma Anniversaries and Holidays

Some trauma survivors are particularly susceptible to time cues that trigger memories or a reexperiencing of the trauma. Sometimes, they may not consciously connect the day or season to their trauma until after symptoms appear. They might be moody and withdrawn or overly anxious and weepy without knowing why at first. Then they might realize it is the anniversary of the rape, the accident, the shooting, the death, or the battle.

Depending on how they're handled, trauma anniversaries can be cause for tension and fear, or an occasion for meaning and connection. Survivors who don't take the time to connect their reactions to an anniversary may hurry to numb or escape their feelings and memories. They might turn to alcohol or other drugs, explode with an anger you hadn't seen in months, or become withdrawn again.

Ask your loved one what would be most helpful. Some trauma survivors may want to do something special to honor the day and the fact that they survived the event. Some may want to spend it in the company of other survivors or go to a recovery meeting if they suffer from dual disorders. Others may not want to think about the trauma and may opt for distraction instead. Some survivors may want to take a quiet walk or a long bath. Survivors of disasters like Katrina or terrorist attacks like 9/11 or the Oklahoma City bombing may want to participate in a public ceremony, visit a memorial, or work on some social service project related to the incident.

Take your own feelings and needs into consideration, too, on trauma anniversaries, since you have also been living with—and reliving—the trauma. Ideally, such times can be opportunities for healthy communication.

Our lives changed on October 16—the day my wife got attacked—and even though it's been five years, we both get so sad around that time. Now we're more intentional about it and use the day to celebrate the fact that we're together, we're in love, and we're both healing. I try to remember to get her flowers or something

she'll enjoy, and we reserve the day just for us—doing something
fun and distracting. Sometimes we'll go see a comedy and out for
dinner. One year we went bowling with friends.

• • •

My nephews were preteens when their big brother died of cancer,
and my sister was very conscious of how left out they probably
felt during his illness when he was—understandably—the focus
of attention. On the first anniversary of his death, she asked the
boys if they wanted to help spread his ashes. The whole family
brainstormed about all his favorite places, then they took a drive
to visit all those places. Afterwards, each got to choose one special
activity for himself and the family did that. Now it's become a
tradition. They talk about their brother, but it is also a day on
which they get extra TLC and attention.

There is no specific anniversary of Michael's trauma, since his
PTSD is related to several events during his tour of duty. But
Veterans Day is a difficult day for him because of the public focus
on war. We begin the day softly with hugs, and sometimes tears,
then he goes to a quiet ceremony with his Vets for Peace group
during which they ring a bell to remember and honor those who
gave—and give—their lives to war and to meditate on peace. He
always invites me to go with, and some years I do, but there are
years when war is too much with me, and I need to do something
totally unrelated to it. At those times, we talk about how each
of us is feeling, and we respect each other's needs and decisions
without defensiveness or guilt. Being intentional about Veterans
Day gives us a way to check in with each other—to measure and
celebrate just how far we've come in our respective journeys of
healing.

We found that approaching the holidays with this same intention-
ality can nip a lot of problems in the bud. Holidays like Christmas,
Hanukkah, New Year's, or Thanksgiving can be filled with stress and

powerful emotions for any of us who celebrate them, but they can be minefields for trauma survivors. I suspect it's difficult to feel warm and fuzzy around a decorated tree that reminds you of how your father got drunk every Christmas Eve and usually came home to beat your mother. I imagine it's painful to watch all the television ads in which happy children are showered with expensive toys and tables are set for feasts when you've lost your job and can't pay this month's mortgage, let alone buy holiday gifts or treats.

Trauma survivors can get nervous or depressed in the midst of crowds or at lively parties where they are expected to be jolly and carefree. If Michael doesn't want to go to a holiday party, I'm getting better at going alone or with a friend, or we'll develop an escape plan ahead of time if either of us is uncertain about going.

It's easy to be filled with apprehension and dread about visiting families during holidays. (Maybe *this* year we'll get through a family meal without fighting. Maybe *this* year Uncle Ted won't get drunk. Maybe *this* year Mom won't pressure me to eat and eat and eat.) Meanwhile, networks broadcast idealistic portraits of happy and harmonious families gathered together in the spirit of love and charity. We forget that these are actors who get paid well to emulate domestic tranquility. When our experience doesn't match their portrayal, we risk feeling let down, anxious, depressed, or lonely. Worse yet, we might be tempted to take a drink, medicate our worries, overeat, or engage in some other unhealthy behavior to dull our misery or emptiness.

As lovely as some traditions may be, we don't have to be held captive by unhealthy holiday routines that make us miserable or threaten to trigger post-traumatic symptoms. If you or your loved one dread holidays, consider trying out new traditions. You may want to serve meals for the homeless on Christmas or host an alcohol-free party. You may opt out of a tension-filled family gathering and choose to meet with friends instead. One year, our group of friends decided to reduce the pressure of gift exchanges agreeing that no one could spend more than five dollars on a gift and that the gift had to come from a second-hand store. We've also chosen to donate money to a charity instead of giving expensive gifts to each other.

You may want to engage in some respectful negotiation if there are some traditions you and your children wish to continue but your loved one finds too painful or likely to trigger post-traumatic symptoms. You may love how your father always strung lights on your house and rigged up outdoor speakers that played holiday music. Your loved one, however, might struggle with hypervigilance, and view a brightly lit house and music as a dangerous target. A compromise might be to let go of your need to decorate your own house and, instead, set aside a night on which you and the kids take a special drive to view holiday lights and decorations on other houses.

Holidays offer many opportunities to practice self-care skills. When we rebuild our lives after a loved one's trauma, we recognize we can make healthier choices—not just during the holidays but also throughout each day of every year.

Into the Light

The quote from James Baldwin at the beginning of this chapter reminds me of the abstract painting over our fireplace mantel titled "Coming Into the Light." A dear cousin of Michael's called it her grief piece when she painted it after her son's tragic death. Steve, twenty-eight years old and ten months sober, was riding with friends in his AA motorcycle group when a truck driver, blinded by the light of the February sun, collided with his bike. Steve died the next morning.

Without our faith in God, our love for each other, and people around us, my husband and I surely would have folded. We had recently enjoyed the musical Les Misérables, *and we played the song "Bring Him Home" every evening as we sat watching the lights dance on the lake outside our home. The most soothing thing we did, besides holding each other in embrace, was listening to that song while the pain flowed like a river down our faces. Steve's ashes were in the lake and we were sure that he was already over the dam and into the ocean. He was not to be contained. For months and even a year after his death, we often saw different young women—Steve's friends—by the lake, floating a single flower.*

The predominant dark blue, tornado-like spirals in the painting remind me of a tumultuous ocean. For me, the calmer pastel swirls that emerge from the darkness toward a small piece of white light represent determined movement through despair into hope and possibility. It is the journey from trauma to healing. It is the journey from acknowledgement to action.

As rabbi and author Harold S. Kushner proclaims, "bad things happen to good people." Trauma happens because this world is unpredictable and imperfect. No matter how strong the levees, hurricanes rage and floods come. No matter how strong the family, trauma can still strike. We can mourn, but we cannot change the reality of trauma. Yet we still have choices about how we interpret experiences, and how we integrate them into our current reality.

Viktor E. Frankl, M.D., Ph.D., was an Austrian neurologist, psychiatrist, and survivor of the Nazi death camps during World War II. In his book *Man's Search for Meaning*, Frankl concluded that everything can be taken from us except one thing: "the last of human freedoms—to choose one's own attitude in any given set of circumstances, to choose one's own way."

Frankl noted that the prisoners most likely to survive were those who had a vivid sense of purpose in life. Even in the humiliation of the camps, prisoners still had choices about how to act. Some betrayed their fellow inmates and secretly allied with German guards. Others committed acts of daily heroism, everything from sharing a last crust of bread to caring for the sick.

Ultimately, courage is about this willingness and capacity to choose. And even in the most arduous circumstances, two choices are almost always available to us: where to place our attention and what action to take next.

Most times these actions are small, deliberate, and slow, and that's just fine because they still indicate *movement*. This movement isn't usually linear; it's often more of a spiral that circles forward as we progress on the path of healing.

We may encounter momentary setbacks when our loved one's symptoms are triggered or we face an unforeseen challenge, but the more we practice good self-care, the more manageable those setbacks might be. It is a slow, deliberate, and ongoing process. As we move from shadows to glimmers of light, even baby steps count. Even the smallest successes deserve to be noted and celebrated—as they are at the Web site www.ptsdforum.org, where there is a place for trauma survivors and those who care for them to record even little victories, which are applauded by other contributors:

> *I am proud of my husband for getting out of bed each morning just so he can be a part of my life. I am proud of myself for not being afraid to ask for help when I don't know what to do to.*

> • • •

> *I can now sleep for more than three or four hours at a time! I am smiling more. Despite some depressive episodes, I am smiling and feeling happy more often.*

> • • •

> *My mother is completely bed and wheelchair bound. She is unable to stand and I am caring for her every need 24/7. I have been stressed to my limit and beyond and yet I am still standing. I am tired and completely exhausted, but I have not crumbled.*

> • • •

> *It's been thirteen years, but I got up the courage to return to the scene of the crash with my wife and kids. There was no sign of what had happened, and I felt serene.*

> • • •

For the past two years, it has always been me who has had to take care of everything, as my husband hasn't had the confidence to do this. But yesterday, my husband stood up for me!

• • •

I actually went out with friends last night—a big accomplishment for me. And I even sang two karaoke songs, even though I had anxiety. I couldn't breathe very well, but I sang both songs all the way through.

Too often, we focus on what we haven't done or couldn't accomplish because we feel exhausted or overwhelmed by all the difficulties and responsibilities that arise in conjunction with our loved one's trauma and post-traumatic symptoms. Instead of overlooking the little accomplishments you and your loved one have made so far, pause for a moment to acknowledge your progress. This is evidence of growth and healing.

When we are in the midst of dealing with the spillover effects of a loved one's trauma, it is common to get engulfed in what a friend calls "heaviosity"—periods filled with dark and serious moments. This can feel like hibernation as we numb and isolate ourselves to the world outside our dark caves. But eventually we have the urge and energy to peek outside, where a bit of sun shines through the fog, reigniting our hope and curiosity.

CELEBRATE YOUR SUCCESSES—HOWEVER SMALL

When we hear the word *success,* most of us probably think of fame or fortune. However, throughout history poets have written about how real satisfaction comes from gifts of the heart— from love and laughter, beauty and song, from doing our best to make the world a better place by raising healthy children or being the best individuals we can be.

Recount the moments you laughed or played or smiled. Was there a time when you paused to notice a flower or a sunset? Did you exchange a word or gesture of affection with another person or smile with a child? Did you and your loved one share a time free of worry or concerns related to trauma?

These are successes worth celebrating. This is movement. This is growth. How can you reward yourself or your family for the progress you continue to make?

Stronger in the Broken Places

It's funny: I always imagined when I was a kid that adults had some kind of inner toolbox, full of shiny tools: the saw of discernment, the hammer of wisdom, the sandpaper of patience. But then when I grew up I found that life handed you these rusty bent old tools—friendships, prayer, conscience, honesty—and said, do the best you can with these, they will have to do. And mostly, against all odds, they're enough.

—Anne Lamott,
Traveling Mercies

I know my family's story is not your story, and your path to healing may not parallel my own, but I've shared my rusty tools with you with the sincere hope that they give you some comfort and provide some ideas you may want to try in your own journey. While each path is different, those who have been touched by trauma do—at some level—travel together.

This book's introduction mentioned the Ernest Hemingway quote, "The world breaks everyone and afterward many are strong at the broken places," and it seems fitting to repeat it at its conclusion. When I think about growing stronger at the broken places, I think about the

Survivor Tree we saw in Oklahoma City—that wonderful symbol of hope and endurance in the aftermath of trauma.

This American Elm, over 100 years old, was the only shade tree in the parking lot across the street from the Murrah Building. The force of the bomb blast ripped most of the branches. Glass and debris were embedded in its trunk, and fire from the cars parked beneath it blackened what was left of the tree. Most thought it wouldn't survive, but almost a year after the bombing, when family members, survivors, and rescue workers gathered for a memorial ceremony under the tree, they noticed the old elm was beginning to bloom again.

Thanks to the tender care and attention it has received, the Survivor Tree now thrives, and each year hundreds of seeds are planted and nurtured into saplings that are now growing all over the United States. Saplings were sent to—among other places—Columbine High School after the shooting there, New York City after 9/11, and Virginia Tech after the campus killings.

When Jessica moved back to Minnesota with her beautiful little family, Michael and I sent them a sapling from the Survivor Tree to plant in the yard of their new home. It seemed to us to be the perfect symbol of resilience and hope—and a way for us to further acknowledge and honor the journey of healing we continue to experience. The shock wave effects from a long-ago trauma have scarred and changed us, but our family is rooted and strong—and growing stronger every day.

Please be tender with yourselves as you continue to heal from the shock wave effects from your loved one's trauma. Seek the help you need. Rest, breathe, love, cry, and laugh, remembering we can be containers for all of it—all at the same time. And as you place one determined foot in front of the other on this journey through the shadows and challenges of trauma, take heart from the voices on these pages and know you do not walk alone.

Resources and Reading

The following is a list of books and places that readers might find interesting or helpful. National organizations can often link you to local agencies. Resources are grouped into three sections: Trauma and PTSD, Self-Care, and Families and Children.

Trauma and PTSD
Catherall, Don R. *Back From the Brink: A Family Guide to Overcoming Traumatic Stress.* New York: Bantam Books, 1992. (Also downloadable at www.emotionalsafety.net/development/families_trauma.htm.)
A thorough overview of the far-reaching effects of PTSD that offers practical advice for trauma survivors and families.

Goulston, Mark. *Post-Traumatic Stress Disorder for Dummies.* Hoboken, NJ: Wiley, 2008.
A very helpful, easy-to-understand reference and overview for survivors of PTSD and their families.

National Center for PTSD (www.ptsd.va.gov)
Helpful information about trauma and PTSD for survivors, families, and professionals.

National Child Traumatic Stress Network (www.nctsnet.org)
Provides information and links on trauma and children and how to best help them.

National Institute of Mental Health, "PTSD" (www.nimh.nih.gov/health/topics/post-traumatic-stress-disorder-ptsd/index.shtml). Good information on trauma and how adults and children can cope with violence and disasters. You can download the helpful booklet "What Parents Can Do" from this Web site.

Mason, Patience H. C. *Recovering from the War: A Woman's Guide to Helping Your Vietnam Vet, Your Family, and Yourself.* New York: Viking Press, 1990.
An informative resource for veterans and their families, written by the wife of a Vietnam combat vet.

Matsakis, Aphrodite. *Vietnam Wives: Facing the Challenges of Life with Veterans Suffering Post-Traumatic Stress.* 2nd ed. Baltimore: Sidran Press, 1996.
Although written for the families of veterans, this is a very helpful and informative book for anyone dealing with the effects of trauma.

Post-Traumatic Gazette (www.patiencepress.com)
Patience Mason, wife of a Vietnam combat vet, provides tons of information about trauma and PTSD in newsletters and brochures—many of which are free and easily downloaded.

PTSD Forum (www.ptsdforum.org)
Support and information for survivors and families affected by trauma.

Shay, Jonathan. *Achilles in Vietnam: Combat Trauma and the Undoing of Character.* New York: Touchstone, Simon & Schuster, 1994.
A fascinating book that traces the history of PTSD and psychological effects of war by comparing the experiences of soldiers in Homer's *Iliad* with those of Vietnam veterans.

Self-Care

Addiction and Recovery
12Step.org is a clearinghouse for information about recovery. Look for links to online meeting schedules and resources for finding local face-to-face meetings.

Adult Children of Alcoholics (www.adultchildren.org)
A Twelve Step organization for men and women who grew up in alcoholic or otherwise dysfunctional homes.

Al-Anon (www.al-anon.alateen.org): 1-888-4AL-ANON (1-888-425-2666)
A Twelve Step organization for loved ones of chemically dependent people.

Alcoholics Anonymous (www.aa.org)
A Twelve Step organization for substance abusers.

Beattie, Melody. *Codependent No More: How to Stop Controlling Others and Start Caring for Yourself.* Center City, MN: Hazelden, 1987, 1992.
The "Bible" of codependency by the author who coined the term.

Beattie, Melody. *Playing It by Heart: Taking Care of Yourself No Matter What.* Center City, MN: Hazelden, 1999.
Personal essays and guidance about codependency.

Nar-Anon (www.nar-anon.org)
A Twelve Step organization for loved ones of addicts.

Realistic Recovery (http://realisticrecovery.wordpress.com)
A variety of information about addiction and recovery by a "nontheist."

Substance Abuse & Mental Health Services Administration (SAMHSA) (www.samhsa.gov)
Government agency that provides good information and links on mental health and substance abuse.

SAMHSA Substance Abuse Treatment Facility Locator (www .findtreatment.samhsa.gov)
Connects individuals to treatment facilities in their area.

Domestic Violence/Rape/Abuse
Benedict, Helen. *The Lonely Soldier: The Private War of Women Serving in Iraq.* Boston: Beacon Press, 2009.
A journalist tells the stories of five women veterans who are survivors of military sexual trauma.

Francisco, Patricia Weaver. *Telling: A Memoir of Rape and Recovery.* New York: HarperCollins, 1999.
An exquisite and brave memoir by a survivor of rape.

National Center on Domestic and Sexual Violence(www.ncdsv.org)
Information on domestic violence and sexual abuse.

National Domestic Violence Hotline (www.ndvh.org)
A national nonprofit organization that provides crisis intervention, information, and referrals to victims of domestic violence, perpetrators, friends, and families. (If you think your computer use might be monitored, you can call the hotline at 1-800-799-7233.)

National Sexual Assault Hotline: 1-800-656-HOPE
(1-800-656-4673, Ext. 1)
A partnership of more than 1,100 local rape treatment hotlines that provides free, confidential services around the clock. Since it began in 1994, the hotline has helped more than one million sexual assault victims.

Rape, Abuse and Incest National Network (RAINN) (www.rainn.org)
RAINN is the nation's largest organization offering help to victims of sexual assault. It provides information for rape and incest victims, the media, policymakers, and other concerned individuals. RAINN's specially trained crisis counselors offer free, anonymous, and completely confidential help 24/7. In addition, the Online Hotline Web site (www.rainn.org/get-help/national-sexual-assault-online-hotline) provides a library of information about recovery, medical issues, and the criminal justice process.

Grief and Loss

Ellis, Thomas M. *This Thing Called Grief: New Understandings of Loss.* Minneapolis: Syren, 2006.
A small and helpful book by a marriage and family therapist with good tips on dealing with grief and loss.

Greenspan, Miriam. *Healing through the Dark Emotions: The Wisdom of Grief, Fear, and Despair.* Boston: Shambhala, 2003.
A gorgeous book written by a psychotherapist who contends that to heal we must feel and work through emotions like grief, fear, and despair, rather than bury or ignore them.

Mental Health/Suicide

American Psychological Association (www.apa.org/helpcenter)
Good information on how and where to find a psychologist in your area.

Baldwin, Christina. *Life's Companion: Journal Writing as a Spiritual Quest.* New York: Bantam, 1990.
A lovely book with many journal exercises to enhance spiritual growth.

Burns, David D. *Feeling Good: The New Mood Therapy.* Revised and updated by David D. Burns. New York: Avon, 1999.
Burns offers ways to develop a positive outlook that help you feel better about yourself and your life.

Cameron, Julia. *The Artist's Way: A Spiritual Path to Higher Creativity.* New York: Jeremy P. Tarcher/Perigee, 1992.
A twelve-week self-study course to ignite your creativity and enhance your spiritual growth.

Chödrön, Pema. *The Places That Scare You: A Guide to Fearlessness in Difficult Times.* Boston: Shambhala, 2005.
An American Buddhist nun offers insights and guidance on how to integrate—rather than deny—the painful aspects of our lives.

Mental Health America (www.mentalhealthamerica.net)
Provides free information on depression, its treatment, and local screening sites.

National Mental Health Association (www.depression-screening.org)
A confidential screening for depression that helps people determine if they should seek medical help.

National Suicide Prevention Lifeline: 1-800-273-8255
A twenty-four-hour hotline staffed by trained counselors, available to anyone in suicidal or emotional distress or for concerned family and friends. Counselors can also provide information about mental health services in your area.

Families and Children
Administration for Children and Families (www.acf.hhs.gov)
Provides information on federal economic and social programs to assist families. You can also find your state's office of child enforcement by checking this Web site, and get current information about laws regarding child support.

Bradshaw, John. *Bradshaw On: The Family—A New Way of Creating Solid Self-Esteem.* Rev. ed. Deerfield Beach, FL: Health Communications, Inc., 1996.
Using family research and recovery principles, Bradshaw discusses ways to heal from dysfunctional family systems.

Clarke, Jean Illsley. *Self-Esteem: A Family Affair.* Minneapolis: Winston Press, 1978.
Clarke maintains that self-esteem starts at home in the nurturing interaction between children and adults, and she offers creative ways to help all family members build their individual self-esteem.

Connect for Kids (www.connectforkids.org).
An online community that provides articles by experts, resources and links to national organizations, a weekly publication of current news and issues that deal with children and families, and an opportunity for online discussion.

Elkind, David. *All Grown Up and No Place to Go: Teenagers in Crisis.* Rev. ed. Cambridge, MA: Perseus, Da Capo Press, 1998.
The Hurried Child: Growing Up Too Fast Too Soon. Cambridge, MA: Da Capo Press, 2007.
The Hurried Child is the twenty-fifth anniversary edition of a landmark book by Elkind, a professor of child study at Tufts University who tackles the problems of children and teens as they struggle to cope in a turbulent society.

Hazelden's *Roots and Wings* Parenting Program
Call Hazelden at 1-800-257-7800 for information on this parenting program.

Hazelden. *Today's Gift: Daily Meditations for Families.* Center City, MN: Hazelden, 1985.
A daily meditation book designed to help family members talk about their thoughts and feelings.

Military One Source (www.militaryonesource.com)
Department of Defense site that offers around-the-clock support
and information for families and soldiers.

National Child Abuse Hotline: 1-800-4-ACHILD
(1-800-422-4453)
Call for help if you are being abused, if you know a child is being
abused, or if you are committing abuse and know you need help.

Office of Safe and Drug-Free Schools
Visit www.ed.gov/offices/OSDFS/parents_guide/title.html
to obtain a free copy of *Growing Up Drug-Free: A Parent's Guide to
Prevention.*

Operation Military Kids (www.operationmilitarykids.org)
The U.S. Army's collaborative effort with America's communities to
support the children and youth impacted by deployment.

United Way Information Site (www.211.org)
Connects people to social services in their area.

Mentoring Programs
Big Brothers/Big Sisters (www.bbbs.org)
Founded in 1904, this is the nation's oldest and largest youth men-
toring organization, with programs in all fifty states.

National Mentoring Partnership (www.mentoring.org)
A national organization that offers training and information to
communities, schools, businesses, civic associations, and churches
that want to establish mentor programs.

Your Time—Their Future (http://ncadi.samhsa.gov/yourtime)
A Substance Abuse and Mental Health Services (SAMSHA)
campaign that features mentoring and volunteer opportunities for
adults.

Bibliography

Al-Anon Family Group Headquarters. "Are You Troubled by Someone's Drinking? Al-Anon Is for You!" Al-Anon/ Alateen. www.al-anon.alateen.org/S17web.html.

American Psychiatric Association. *Diagnostic and Statistical Manual of Mental Disorders.* 4th ed., text rev. Washington, DC: American Psychiatric Association, 2000.

Baldwin, Christina. *Life's Companion: Journal Writing as a Spiritual Quest.* New York: Bantam, 1990.

———. *Storycatcher: Making Sense of Our Lives through the Power and Practice of Story.* Novato, CA. New World Library, 2005.

——— and Cynthia Orange. *New Life, New Friends: Making and Keeping Relationships in Recovery.* New York: Random House, Bantam, 1993.

Baldwin, James. "Nothing Personal." *The Blues Vision,* Volume 6, Article 4, 1983. Contributions in Black Studies. The Berkeley Electronic Press. http://scholarworks.umass.edu/cibs.

Beattie, Melody. *Codependent No More: How to Stop Controlling*

Others and Start Caring for Yourself. Center City, MN: Hazelden, 1987, 1992.

Bentley, Steve. "A Short History of PTSD: From Thermopylae to Hue, Soldiers Have Always Had a Disturbing Reaction to War." *The VVA Veteran* (March/April 2005). www.vva.org/archive/TheVeteran/2005_03/feature_HistoryPTSD.htm.

Berry, Wendell. "The Peace of Wild Things." In *The Selected Poems of Wendell Berry.* Berkeley, CA: Counterpoint, 1999.

Bodhi. "A Buddhist's Non-Theist 12 Steps." Realistic Recovery. http://realisticrecovery.wordpress.com/2009/05/29/a-buddhists-non-theist-12-steps.

Bradshaw, John. *Bradshaw On: The Family—A New Way of Creating Solid Self-Esteem.* Rev. ed. Deerfield Beach, FL: Health Communications, Inc., 1996.

Breen, J. Colleen. *Making Changes: A Guidebook for Managing Life's Challenges.* Minneapolis: Fairview Press, 1995. (Interview with author, July 6, 2006.)

Bremner, J. Douglas. "Acute and Chronic Responses to Psychological Trauma: Where Do We Go from Here?" *American Journal of Psychiatry* 156 (March 1999). http://ajp.psychiatryonline.org/cgi/content/full/156/3/349.

Burns, David D. *Feeling Good: The New Mood Therapy.* Revised and updated by David D. Burns. New York: Avon, 1999.

Cameron, Julia. *The Artist's Way: A Spiritual Path to Higher Creativity.* New York: Jeremy P. Tarcher/Perigee, 1992.

Casey, Karen. *Each Day a New Beginning.* Center City, MN: Hazelden, 1982.

Catherall, Don R. *Back From the Brink: A Family Guide to Overcoming Traumatic Stress.* New York: Bantam, 1992. (Also downloadable at www.emotionalsafety.net/development/families_trauma.htm.)

Clarke, Jean Illsley. *Self-Esteem: A Family Affair.* Minneapolis: Winston Press, 1978.

Dickson, Charles. "Learning Human Relations from Geese." *The American Legion Magazine,* December 1999.

Ellis, Thomas M. *This Thing Called Grief: New Understandings of Loss.* Minneapolis: Syren, 2006.

Engs, Ruth C. "Addictive Behaviors and the Addictive Process." (Adapted from Engs, R. C. *Alcohol and Other Drugs: Self Responsibility.* Bloomington, IN: Tichenor Publishing Company, 1987). www.indiana.edu/~engs/hints/addictiveb.html.

Evans, Katie, and J. Michael Sullivan. *Treating Addicted Survivors of Trauma.* New York: Guilford Press, 1995.

Francisco, Patricia Weaver. *Telling: A Memoir of Rape and Recovery.* New York: HarperCollins, 1999.

Frankl, Viktor E. *Man's Search for Meaning.* New York: Pocket Books, Simon & Schuster, 1985.

Friedman, Matthew J. "Posttraumatic Stress Disorder: An Overview." United States Department of Veterans Affairs,

National Center for PTSD. www.ptsd.va.gov/professional/ pages/ptsd-overview.asp.

Fulghum, Robert L. *All I Really Need to Know I Learned in Kindergarten: Uncommon Thoughts on Uncommon Things.* New York: Random House, Ballantine, 1986, 1988.

Garbarino, James. *Lost Boys: Why Our Sons Turn Violent and How We Can Save Them.* New York: Simon & Schuster, The Free Press, 1999.

Gordon, Thomas. "A Credo for My Relationships with Others." www.gordontraining.com/A_Credo_for_Your_Relationships_ with_Others.html.

Greenspan, Miriam. *Healing through the Dark Emotions: The Wisdom of Grief, Fear, and Despair.* Boston: Shambhala, 2003.

Hazelden. *Roots and Wings Handbook: Raising Resilient Children Parent's Handbook.* Rev. ed. Center City, MN: Hazelden, 2000.

————. *What to Say or Do . . . From Diapers to Diploma: A Parents' Quick Reference Guide.* Minneapolis: Johnson Institute, 1998; reprint, with an introduction by Kay Provine, Center City, MN: Hazelden, 2000.

Helpguide.org. "Understanding Stress: Signs, Symptoms, Causes, and Effects." www.helpguide.org/mental/stress_signs.htm.

Henry J. Kaiser Family Foundation. "Children and the News: Coping with Terrorism, War and Everyday Violence." www.kff. org/entmedia/upload/Key-Facts-Children-and-the-News.pdf.

Herman, Judith Lewis. *Trauma and Recovery.* New York: Basic Books, 1992.

In All Our Affairs: Making Crises Work for You. Virginia Beach, VA: Al-Anon Family Groups, 1990.

Kunzman, Kristin. *The Healing Way: Adult Recovery from Childhood Sexual Abuse.* San Francisco: Harper & Row, 1990, (A Hazelden Book).

Kushner, Harold S. *When Bad Things Happen to Good People.* New York: Avon, 1981.

Lamott, Anne. *Traveling Mercies: Some Thoughts on Faith.* New York: Anchor, 1999.

Lovell, Philip, and Julia Isaacs. "The Impact of the Mortgage Crisis on Children." www.firstfocus.net/Download/HousingandChildrenFINAL.pdf.

Matsakis, Aphrodite. *Vietnam Wives: Facing the Challenges of Life with Veterans Suffering Post-Traumatic Stress.* 2nd ed. Baltimore: Sidran Press, 1996.

National Child Traumatic Stress Network. "What Is Child Traumatic Stress?" www.nctsn.org/nctsn_assest/pdfs/what_is_child_traumatic_stess.pdf.

National Institute of Mental Health (NIMH). *Helping Children and Adolescents Cope With Violence and Disasters: What Parents Can Do.* www.nimh.nih.gov/health/publications/helping-children-and-adolescents-cope-with-violence-and-disasters-what-parents-can-do/index.shtml.

National Mental Health Association. "Disaster and Your Mental Health: What Is a Normal Response, and When to Seek Help." www.mhamc.org/html/downloads/pdf/Disaster%20

and%20Your%20Mental%20Health%20When%20to%20
Seek%20Help.pdf.

National Suicide Prevention Lifeline. "What Are the Warning
Signs for Suicide?" www.suicidepreventionlifeline.org/GetHelp/
SuicideWarningSigns.aspx.

Neruda, Pablo. "If each day falls . . . ." In *The Sea and the Bells*.
Translated by William O'Daly. Port Townsend, WA: Copper
Canyon Press. Copyright © 1973 by Pablo Neruda and the
Heirs of Pablo Neruda. Translation copyright © 1988, 2002 by
William O'Daly.

Orange, Cynthia. *Sing Your Own Song: A Guide for Single Moms*.
Center City, MN: Hazelden, 2001.

Paige, Stephen R. "What Is Post-traumatic Stress Disorder
(PTSD)?" EMedicineHealth. www.emedicinehealth.com/
post-traumatic_stress_disorder_ptsd/article_em.htm.

Posttraumatic Stress Disorder DSM IV Diagnosis & Criteria.
"309.81 Posttraumatic Stress." www.mental-health-today.com/
ptsd/dsm.htm.

Price, Jennifer L. "Children of Veterans and Adults with PTSD."
U.S. Department of Veterans Affairs, National Center for
PTSD. http://ncptsd.va.gov/ncmain/ndocs/fac_shts/fs_
children_veterans.html?opm=1&rr=rr112&srt=d&echorr=true.

PTSD Forum. www.ptsdforum.org.

Real, Terrence. *I Don't Want to Talk About It: Overcoming the
Secret Legacy of Male Depression*. New York: Fireside/Simon &
Schuster, 1998.

Thorndike, Frances P., Rachel Wernicke, Michelle Y. Pearlman, and David A. F. Haaga. "Nicotine Dependence, PTSD Symptoms, and Depression Proneness Among Male and Female Smokers." National Institutes of Health. www.ncbi.nlm.nih.gov:80/pmc/articles/PMC1513639.

United States Department of Veterans Affairs, National Center for PTSD. "Anger and Trauma," www.ptsd.va.gov/public/pages/anger-and-trauma.asp.

———. "Helping a Family Member Who Has PTSD," www.ptsd.va.gov/public/pages/helping-family-member.asp.

———. "How Common is PTSD?" www.ptsd.va.gov/public/pages/how-common-is-ptsd.asp.

———. "Aging Veterans and Posttraumatic Stress Symptoms." www.ptsd.va.gov/public/pages/ptsd-older-vets.asp.

———. "PTSD and Problems with Alcohol Use." www.ptsd.va.gov/public/pages/ptsd-alcohol-use.asp.

———. "PTSD and Your Family." www.ptsd.va.gov/public/pages/ptsd-and-your-family.asp.

About the Author

CYNTHIA ORANGE HAS WRITTEN EXTENSIVELY about addiction and recovery, parenting, and post-traumatic stress disorder. She co-facilitates a caregivers' support group, and she and her husband (a Vietnam combat veteran) often speak to audiences about the effects of trauma and war in their continuing involvement with veterans and veterans' issues. She is an award-winning writer who has published hundreds of articles, columns, and guest editorials in newspapers, magazines, and literary journals. She is the author of several books, and contributed to the popular meditation book *Today's Gift*.